THE ART OF
HORSEMANSHIP

The Art of Horsemanship

XENOPHON

Edited and Translated by
MORRIS H. MORGAN

Proficies nihil hoc, caedas licet usque, flagello.

Illustrated

DOVER PUBLICATIONS, INC.
Mineola, New York

Bibliographical Note

This Dover edition, first published in 2006, is an unabridged republication of the work originally published by Little, Brown and Company, Boston, 1893.

International Standard Book Number

ISBN-13: 978-0-486-44753-7
ISBN-10: 0-486-44753-7

Manufactured in the United States by Courier Corporation
44753703
www.doverpublications.com

PREFACE.

AMONG technical treatises, that of Xenophon on Horsemanship is almost unique in
one particular. Even after more than twenty-
three centuries it is still, in the main, a
sound and excellent guide for so much of the
field as it covers. This fact, together with
the simple and delightful manner in which
the subject is treated, has led me to think
that some who are not able or do not care
to approach the book in the original Greek,
might like to read a translation of the earliest known work on the horse and how to
ride him. To be sure, there have already
been versions in English; but these seem to
me, and have seemed to others, unsatisfactory.

My translation is made from the Greek
text of Dindorf's Oxford edition. Two
well-known special editions of the treatise I

have found very useful. These are by
Courier, with notes and a translation into
French, first published in Paris in 1813, and
by Jacobs, with notes and a German version,
Gotha, 1825. Hermann's essay, " De verbis
quibus Graeci incessum equorum indicant,"
is indispensable for the study of certain parts
of the treatise. I have also consulted the
German translation of Ginzrot, with brief
notes, in the second volume of his large
work called " Die Wagen und Fuhrwerke
der Griechen und Römer," Munich, 1817.
Ginzrot's book must be used with caution;
the illustrations are often fanciful, and the
statements need verification; but his translation of Xenophon is sometimes helpful. In
English I have seen three translations, —
Berenger's (in his " History and Art of Horsemanship," London, 1771, a somewhat rare
book, for the loan of which I am obliged to
the Librarian of the Boston Athenaeum); an
anonymous translation reprinted with the
minor works of Xenophon in Philadelphia in
1845; and Watson's, in Bohn's Classical
Library. The first is by far the best, but I
have not found either of the three of much

assistance. There has been no edition of the Greek text with English notes.

The illustrations in this book are all selected from the antique, and are reproduced from the best sources at my command. These sources, together with a brief description of each picture, are given on page 158 ff. I might have illustrated almost every subject in the treatise by means of the Parthenon frieze; but I choose rather to omit all but a few of these well-known works, and to present others which are less generally known to the readers for whom my book is primarily intended. For it will be easy to see that I have not written for philologians. The brief essay on the Greek Riding-horse makes no pretence to completeness, and little to originality. In it, and in the notes which follow, my chief intention has been to offer only what I thought would be necessary explanation or interesting information to those who do not profess to be classical scholars. Yet perhaps even such scholars may find here and there, especially in the notes, a few points which may be new, and, I hope, not unacceptable to them. And I sincerely wish that this little book might lead some one to a more thorough study of the subjects of riding and driving in antiquity. They offer a fertile and interesting field for special investigation.

Besides the German works already mentioned, and the ordinary classical handbooks, the best books in which to find information about the Greek horse and horsemanship are Schlieben's "Die Pferde des Altertums," 1867, Martin's "Les Cavaliers Athéniens," 1886, and Daremberg and Saglio's "Dictionnaire des Antiquités," under the words *equites*, *equus*, etc. I have not seen Lehndorf's "Hippodromos," 1876, nor Piétrement's "Les chevaux dans les temps historiques et préhistoriques," 1883. One of the most charming of the works of Cherbuliez is his "Cheval de Phidias," 1864, in which the subject is considered from purely artistic and aesthetic points of view. Of course there is much information scattered through periodical literature; but, in spite of all, the book of the ancient horse is yet to be written.

M. H. M.

May, 1893.

CONTENTS.

———◆———

XENOPHON ON HORSEMANSHIP.

CHAPTER I.

IT has been my fortune to spend a great deal of time in riding, and so I think myself versed in the horseman's art. This makes me willing to set forth to the younger of my friends what I believe would be the best way for them to deal with horses. It is true that a book on horsemanship has already been written by Simon:[1] I mean the man who dedicated the bronze horse at the Eleusinion[2] in Athens with his own exploits

[1] The numerals refer to the Notes, p. 119 ff.

in relief on the pedestal. Still, I shall not
strike out of my work all the points in which
I chance to agree with him, but shall take
much greater pleasure in passing them on
to my friends, believing that I speak with
the more authority because a famous horseman, such as he, has thought as I do. And
then, again, I shall try to make clear whatever he has omitted.

To begin with, I shall describe how a
man, in buying a horse, would be least
likely to be cheated. In the case of an
unbroken colt, of course his frame is what
you must test; as for spirit, no very sure
signs of that are offered by an animal that
has never yet been mounted. And in his
frame, the first things which I say you
ought to look at are his feet.[3] Just as a
house would be good for nothing if it were
very handsome above but lacked the proper
foundations, so too a war-horse, even if all his
other points were fine, would yet be good for
nothing if he had bad feet; for he could not
use a single one of his fine points.

The feet should first be tested by examining the horn; thick horn[4] is a much better

mark of good feet than thin. Again, one
should not fail to note whether the hoofs at
toe and heel come up high or lie low. High
ones keep what is called the frog[5] well off
the ground, while horses with low hoofs walk
with the hardest and softest part of the foot
at once, like knock-kneed men. Simon says
that their sound is a proof of good feet, and
he is right; for a hollow hoof resounds like a
cymbal as it strikes the ground.

As we have begun here, let us now proceed
to the rest of the body. The bones above
the hoofs and below the fetlocks should not
be very straight up and down, like the goat's;
for if they have no spring, they jar the rider,
and such legs are apt to get inflamed. These
bones should not come down very low, either,
else the horse might get his fetlocks stripped
of hair[6] and torn in riding over heavy ground
or over stones. The shank bones ought to
be stout, for they are the supporters of the
body; but they should not be thickly coated
with flesh or veins: if they are, in riding over
hard ground the veins would fill with blood
and become varicose, the legs would swell,
and the flesh recede. With this slackening

of the flesh, the back sinew[7] often gives way,
and makes the horse lame. As for the knees,
if they are supple in bending when the colt
walks, you may infer that his limbs will be
supple in riding; for as time goes on, all colts
get more and more supple at the knees.
Supple knees are highly esteemed; and justly,
because they make the horse easier and less
likely to stumble than stiff ones. Forearms[8]
stout below the shoulders look stronger and
comelier, as they do in man.

The broader the chest so much the hand-
somer and the stronger is it, and the more
naturally adapted to carry the legs well apart
and without interference. The neck should
not be thrown out from the chest like a
boar's, but, like a cock's, should rise straight
up to the poll and be slim at the bend,
while the head, though bony, should have
but a small jaw.[9] The neck would then
protect the rider, and the eye see what lies
before the feet. A horse thus shaped could
do the least harm, even if he were very high-
spirited; for it is not by arching the neck
and head, but by stretching them out, that
horses try their powers of violence. You

should note also whether his jaws are fine or hard, whether they are alike or different.[10] Horses whose jaws are unlike are generally hard-mouthed. A prominent eye rather than a sunken one is a sure sign that the horse is wide awake; and such a one can see farther too. Wide nostrils [11] mean freer breathing than close ones, and at the same time they make the horse look fiercer; for whenever a horse is provoked at another or gets excited during exercise, he dilates his nostrils very widely.

A rather large poll [12] and ears somewhat small give the head more of the look which a horse should have. High withers make the rider's seat surer, and his grip on the shoulders stronger. A double back [13] is easier to sit upon, and better looking than a single one. A deep side, rather rounded at the belly, generally makes the horse at once easier to sit upon, stronger, and a better feeder. The broader and the shorter the loins, with so much the greater ease does the horse raise his forehand and bring up the hind-quarters to follow; then, too, the belly looks smallest, which, when it is large, is not only disfiguring, but makes the horse weaker and more unwieldy. The quarters should be broad and full in proportion to the sides and chest; and all these parts, if firm, would be lighter for running, and make your horse a great deal faster. If he has his buttocks well apart under the tail with the line between them broad, he will be sure to spread well behind; in so doing he will have a stronger and a prouder look, both when gathering himself in [14] and in riding, and all his points will be improved. You may take the case of men to prove this; whenever they wish to lift anything from the ground, they do it with their legs apart rather than close together. The horse should certainly not have large stones; but this point cannot be determined in the colt. As for the hocks below, or the shanks and the fetlocks and hoofs, I say about them here just what I did in the case of the forefeet.

I will set down, too, how you are least likely to miss the mark in the matter of size. That colt always turns out the largest whose shanks are longest at the time of foaling. For the shanks do not grow [15] very much in any

quadrupeds as time goes on, but the rest of
the frame grows so as to correspond to the
shanks.   It seems to me that, by testing a
colt's shape in the manner described, people
would get, as a general rule, an animal with
sound feet, strong, good-conditioned, graceful, and large.   Even though some alter as
they grow, we should still apply these tests
with confidence, since there are a great many
more ugly colts that turn out handsome than
handsome ones that turn out ugly.

CHAPTER II.

I T does not seem necessary for me to
describe the method of breaking a colt,
because those who are enlisted in the cavalry [16]
in our states are persons of very considerable
means, and take no small part in the government. It is also a great deal better than
being a horse-breaker for a young man to see
that his own condition and that of his horse
is good, or if he knows this already, to keep
up his practice in riding; while an old man
had better attend to his family and friends, to
public business and military matters, than
be spending his time in horse-breaking.

The man, then, that feels as I do about horse-breaking will, of course, put out his colt. He should not put him out, however, without having a written contract made, stating what the horse is to be taught before he is returned, just as he does when he puts his son out to learn a trade. This will serve as a reminder to the horse-breaker of what he must attend to, if he is to get his fee.

See to it that the colt be kind, used to the hand, and fond of men when he is put out to the horse-breaker. He is generally made so at home and by the groom, if the man knows how to manage so that solitude means to the colt hunger and thirst and teasing horseflies, while food, drink, and relief from pain come from man. For if this be done, colts must not only love men, but even long for them. Then, too, the horse should be stroked in the places which he most likes to have handled; that is, where the hair is thickest, and where he is least able to help himself if anything hurts him. The groom should also be directed to lead him through crowds, and to make him familiar with all sorts of sights and all sorts of noises. Whenever the colt is frightened at any of them, he should be taught, not by irritating but by soothing him, that there is nothing to fear. It seems to me that this is enough to tell the amateur to do in the matter of horse-breaking.

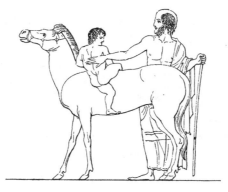

CHAPTER III.

I SHALL now set down some memoranda to be observed in buying a horse already broken to riding, if you are not to be cheated in the purchase. First, then, the question of age should not pass unnoticed; for if he no longer has the markers,[17] the prospect is not a glad one, and he is not to be disposed of so easily. His youth once made sure of, the way in which he lets you put the bit into his mouth, and the head-piece about his ears, should not escape you. This would be least likely to pass unnoticed if the bridle were put on and taken off in the sight

of the purchaser.   Next we ought to observe
how he receives the rider upon his back; a
good many horses hardly let come near them
things whose very approach is a sign that
there is work to be done.   This, too, must
be observed, — whether, when mounted, he
is willing to leave other horses, or whether,
when ridden near horses that are standing
still, he runs away towards them.   Some
horses, also, from bad training take flight
towards home from the riding-grounds.   The
exercise called the Volte [18] shows up a hard
mouth, and even more the practice of changing the direction.   Many horses do not try
to run away unless the mouth is hard on the
same side with the road for a bolt towards
home.[19]   Then you must know whether,
when let out at full speed, he will come
to the poise and be willing to turn round.
It is not a bad thing to try whether he is
just as ready to mind when roused by a blow
as he was before.   A disobedient servant is
of course a useless thing, and so is a disobedient army; a disobedient horse is not
only useless, but he often plays the part of a
very traitor.

As I assume that the horse to be bought is meant for war, trial should be made of all the qualities that war itself puts to the test. These are jumping ditches, going over walls, breasting banks, and leaping down from them; you must try him riding up hill and down dale and along the slope. All these tests prove whether his spirit is strong and his body sound. He should not be rejected, however, if he does not perform them all very finely; as many animals fail, not from inability but from want of practice in these feats. With instruction, habit, and practice they may do all finely, provided they are sound and not vicious. But you must beware of horses that are naturally shy. The over-timid let no harm come to the enemy from off their backs, and they often throw the rider and bring him into the greatest danger.

You must learn, too, whether the horse has any particular vice, shown towards other horses or towards men, and whether he is very skittish. These are all troublesome matters for his owner. You could much better discover objections to being bridled and mounted and other vices, by trying to

do over again, after the horse has finished
his work, just what you did before beginning
your ride.   Horses that are ready to submit
to a task the second time, after having done
it once, give proof enough of high spirit.
To sum it all up, the least troublesome and
the most serviceable to his rider in the wars
would naturally be the horse that is sound-
footed, gentle, sufficiently fleet, ready and
able to undergo fatigue, and, first and fore-
most, obedient.   On the other hand, horses
that need much urging from laziness or much
coaxing and attention from being too mettle-
some, keep the rider's hands always engaged,
and take away his courage in moments of
danger.

CHAPTER IV.

WHEN one has bought a horse that he really admires, and has taken him home, it is a good thing to have his stall [20] in such a part of the establishment that his master shall very often have an eye [21] on the animal; it is well, too, that the stable should be so arranged that the horse's food can no more be stolen out of the manger than his master's out of the storeroom. In my opinion, the man who neglects this matter is neglecting himself; for it is plain that in moments of danger the master gives his own life into the keeping of his horse. A secure stable is a good thing, not only to prevent the stealing of grain, but also because you can easily tell when the horse refuses his feed. Observing this, you may know either that there is too much blood in him, or that he has been overworked and wants rest, or that barley surfeit[22] or some other disease is coming on. In the horse, as in the man, all diseases are easier to cure at the start than after they have become chronic and have been wrongly diagnosed.

The same care which is given to the horse's food and exercise, to make his body grow strong, should also be devoted to keeping his feet in condition. Even naturally sound hoofs get spoiled in stalls with moist, smooth floors. The floors should be sloping, to avoid moisture, and, to prevent smoothness, stones[23] should be sunk close to one another, each about the size of the hoofs. The mere standing on such floors strengthens the feet. Further, of course, the groom should lead the horse out somewhere to rub him down, and should loose him from the manger after breakfast, so that he may go to dinner the more readily. This place outside of the stall would be best suited to the purpose of strengthening the horse's feet if you threw down loosely four or five cartloads of round stones, each big enough to fill your hand and about a pound and a half in weight, surrounding the whole with an iron border to keep them from getting scattered. Standing on these would be as good for him as travelling a stony road for some part of every day; and whether he is being rubbed down or is teased by horseflies, he has to use his hoofs exactly as he does in walking. Stones strewn about in this way strengthen the frogs too. As for his mouth, you must take as much care to make it soft as you take to make his hoofs hard; and the same treatment softens a horse's mouth that softens a man's flesh.[24]

CHAPTER V.

IT is also a horseman's duty, I think, to
see that his groom is taught the proper
way to treat the horse. First of all, he
ought to know that he should never make
the knot in the halter at the place where the
head-piece fits round. The horse often rubs
his head against the manger, and it may
make sores if the halter is not easy about
the ears; and of course when there are sores,
then the horse must be somewhat fretful
in bridling and grooming. It is well that
the groom should have orders to carry out

the droppings and the litter every day to
a given place; by doing so he may get rid of
it in the easiest way for himself, and would be
doing the horse good too. The groom must
understand that he is to put the muzzle [25]
on the horse when he leads him out to be
rubbed down or to the place where he rolls; [26]
in fact, the horse ought always to be muzzled
whenever he is taken anywhere without a
bridle. The muzzle, without hindering his
breathing, allows no biting, and when it is
on, it serves to keep horses from mischievous
designs. The horse should by all means be
fastened from above his head; for instinct
makes him toss his head up when anything
is worrying him about his face, and if he is
fastened in this way, the tossing slackens the
halter instead of pulling it taut.

In grooming, begin with the head and
mane; if the upper parts are not clean, it is
waste labour to clean the lower parts. Next
raise the hair on the rest of the body by the
use of all the ordinary cleaning implements,[27]
and then clear away the dust by working
with the grain of the hair; but the hair on
the backbone should never be touched by

any implement at all. It is to be rubbed with the hand, and softly smoothed in its natural direction; for thus the seat would be least injured. The head, however, must be washed with water; [28] it is bony, and to clean it with iron or wood would hurt the horse. The forelock also should be wetted; this hair, even though pretty long, does not prevent the horse from seeing, but clears away from his eyes things that would hurt them. The gods, we must believe, gave this tuft to the horse instead of the huge ears which they gave to asses and mules to protect their eyes.

The tail and mane should be washed, seeing that the hair must be made to grow on the tail, so that the horse, reaching out as far as possible, may switch away things that torment him, and made to grow on the neck to afford plenty to take hold of in mounting. The mane, forelock, and tail are gifts of the gods bestowed on the horse for beauty.[29] A proof is that brood mares, as long as their hair is flowing, are not so apt to admit asses, whence all breeders of mules cut off the hair [30] from their mares preparatory to covering.

Washing down of the legs is a thing I absolutely forbid; it does no good, — on the contrary, daily washing is bad for the hoofs. And washing under the belly should be done very sparingly; it worries the horse more than washing anywhere else, and the cleaner these parts are made, the more they attract things under the belly that would torment it. And no matter what pains one has spent on it, the horse is no sooner led out than it gets exactly as dirty as before. These parts, then, should be let alone; and as for the legs, rubbing with the mere hand is quite enough.

CHAPTER VI.

NEXT I shall explain how a man may groom a horse with the least danger to himself and the greatest good to the animal. If he tries to clean him facing with the horse, he runs the risk of a blow in the face from knee or hoof; but if he faces just the other way and outside the reach of the leg, when he cleans him, and takes his place off the shoulder-blade in rubbing him down, he will not be harmed at all, and may even bend back the hoof and attend to the horse's frog. Let him clean the hind legs in the same way. The man that takes care of the horse should know that both in this matter and in everything else which has to be done, the very last places at which he should approach to do it are in front and behind;

for if the horse means mischief, these are the
two points at which he has the advantage
of a man. But by approaching him at the
side you can handle him most freely and
with the least danger to yourself.

When a horse is to be led, I certainly do
not approve of leading him behind you; for
then you have the least chance to look out
for yourself, and the horse has the best chance
to do whatever he likes. Then again I object
to teaching the horse to go on ahead with a
long leading-rein. The reason is that the
horse can then do mischief on either side he
pleases, and can even whirl round and face
his leader. Why, only think of several
horses led together in this fashion, — how in
the world could they be kept away from one
another? But a horse that is accustomed to
be led by the side can do the least mischief
to other horses and to men, and would be
most convenient and ready for the rider,
especially if he should ever have to mount
in a hurry.

In order to put the bridle on properly, the
groom should first come up on the near [31] side
of the horse; then, throwing the reins over

the head and letting them drop on the
withers, he should take the head-piece [32] in
his right hand and offer the bit with his left.
If the horse receives it, of course the head-
stall [33] is to be put on; but if he does not
open his mouth, the bit should be held
against his teeth and the thumb of the left
hand thrust within his jaw. This makes most
horses open the mouth. If he does not
receive the bit even then, press his lip hard
against the tush; very few horses refuse it on
feeling this.

Let your groom be well instructed in the
following points: first, never to lead the
horse by one rein,[34] for this makes one side of
the mouth harder than the other; secondly,
what is the proper distance of the bit from
the corners of the mouth: if too close, it
makes the mouth callous, so that it has no
delicacy of feeling; but if the bit hangs too
low down in the mouth, the horse can take it
in his teeth and so refuse to mind it.

The following must also be urged strongly
upon the groom if any work at all is to be
done. Willingness to receive the bit is
such an important point that a horse which

refuses it is utterly useless. Now, if the bridle is put on not only when he is going to be worked, but also when he is led to his food and home after exercise, it would not be at all strange if he should seize the bit of his own accord when you hold it out to him. It is well for the groom to understand how to put a rider up Persian fashion,[35] so that his master, if he gets infirm or has grown oldish, may himself have somebody to mount him handily or may be able to oblige another with a person to mount him.

The one great precept and practice in using a horse is this, — never deal with him when you are in a fit of passion. A fit of passion is a thing that has no foresight in it, and so we often have to rue the day when we gave way to it. Consequently, when your horse shies at an object and is unwilling to go up to it, he should be shown that there is nothing fearful in it, least of all to a courageous horse like him; [36] but if this fails, touch the object yourself that seems so dreadful to him, and lead him up to it with gentleness. Compulsion and blows inspire only the more fear; for when horses are at all hurt at such a time, they think that what they shied at is the cause of the hurt.

I do not find fault with a horse for knowing how to settle down [37] so as to be mounted easily, when the groom delivers him to the rider; still, I think that the true horseman ought to practise and be able to mount even if the horse does not so offer himself. Different horses fall to one's lot at different times, and the same horse serves you one way at one time and another at another.

CHAPTER VII.

I SHALL next set down the method of riding which the horseman may find best for himself and his horse, when once he has received him for mounting. First, then, with the left hand he must take up lightly the halter [38] which hangs from the chin-strap [39] or the noseband, holding it so slack as not to check the horse, whether he intends to raise himself by laying hold of the mane about the ears, [40] and to mount in that way, or whether he vaults on from his spear. [41] With the right hand, he must then take the reins

at the withers and also grasp the mane, so
that he may not wrench the horse's mouth at
all as he gets up. In springing to his place,
he must draw up the body with the left hand,
keeping his right stiff as he raises himself
with it; for in mounting thus, he will not
look ungraceful even from behind. The leg
should be kept bent, the knee must not
touch the horse's back, and the calf must
be brought clean over to the off side. After
having brought his foot completely round, he
is then to settle down in his seat on the
horse. I think it good that the horseman
should practise springing up from the off
side as well, on the chance that he may
happen to be leading his horse with the left
hand and holding his spear in his right. He
has only to learn to do with the left what
he did before with the right, and with the
right what he did with the left. Another
reason why I approve of the latter method
of mounting is that the moment he is on
horseback the rider would be completely
ready, if he should have to engage the enemy
all of a sudden.

When the rider takes his seat, whether

bareback or on the cloth,[42] I do not approve
of a seat which is as though the man were
on a chair, but rather as though he were
standing upright with his legs apart. Thus
he would get a better grip with his thighs
on the horse, and, being upright, he could
hurl his javelin more vigorously and strike
a better blow from on horseback, if need
be. His foot and leg from the knee down
should hang loosely, for if he keeps his leg
stiff and should strike it against something,
he might get it broken; but a supple leg
would yield, if it struck against anything,
without at all disturbing the thigh. Then,
too, the rider should accustom himself to
keep his body above the hips as supple as
possible; for this would give him greater
power of action, and he would be less liable
to a fall if somebody should try to pull or
push him off. The horse should be taught
to stand still when the rider is taking his seat,
and until he has drawn his skirts from under
him, if necessary, made the reins even, and
taken the most convenient grasp of his spear.
Let him then keep his left arm at his side;
this will give the rider the tidiest look, and to

his hand the greatest power. As for reins, I recommend such as are alike, not weak nor slippery and not thick either, so that if necessary the hand may hold the spear as well.

When the horse gets the signal to start, let him begin at a walk, for this frets him least. If the horse carries his head low, hold the reins with the hands a bit high; if he carries it somewhat high, then rather low: this would make the most graceful appearance. Next, by taking the true trot the horse would relax his body with the least discomfort, and come with the greatest ease into the hand gallop. And as leading with the left is the more approved way, this lead would best be reached if the signal to gallop should be given the horse at the moment when he is rising with his right in the trot; for, being about to raise his left foot next, he would lead with it and would begin the stride as he comes over to the left, — for the horse instinctively leads with the right on turning to the right, and with the left on turning to the left.[43]

I recommend the exercise known as the

Volte, because it accustoms the horse to turn on either jaw. Changing the direction is also a good thing, that the jaws on either side may be equally suppled. But I recommend the Career with sharp turns at each end rather than the complete Volte; for the horse would like turning better after he has had enough of the straight course, and thus would be practising straight-away running and turning at the same time. He must be collected at the turns, because it is not easy or safe for the horse to make short turns when he is at full speed, especially if the ground is uneven or slippery. When the rider collects him, he must not throw the horse aslant at all with the bit, nor sit at all aslant himself; else he must be well aware, that a slight matter will be enough to bring himself and his horse to the ground. The moment the horse faces the stretch after finishing the turn, the rider should push him on to go faster. In war, of course, turns are executed for the purpose of pursuing or retreating; hence it is well that he should be trained to speed after turning.

After the horse appears to have had enough

exercise, it is well to give him a rest and then
to urge him suddenly to the top of his speed,
either away from other horses or towards
them; then to quiet him down out of his
speed by pulling him up very short, and
again, after a halt, to turn him and push him
on. It is very certain that there will come
times when each of these manœuvres will be
necessary. When the moment comes to dismount, never do so among other horses, nor
in a crowd of bystanders, nor outside of the
riding-ground; but let the horse enjoy a
season of rest in the very place where he is
obliged to work.

CHAPTER VIII.

THERE are many occasions, of course, when the horse will have to run down hill and up hill and along a slope, as well as to take a leap across or out of something and to jump down. So all these movements must be learned and practised by both horse and rider. The two will thus become obviously the more helpful and useful to one another. If it is thought that I am repeating myself because I am speaking now of what I have spoken before, let me say that there is no repetition here. I did lay down that you should try whether the horse could do all this at the time you bought him; but what I am now urging is that a man should teach his own horse, and I shall describe the right method of instruction.

With a horse that has no experience whatever in leaping, take him with the leading rein loose and leap across the ditch before him; then draw the rein tight to make him jump over. If he refuses, let somebody with a whip or stick lay it on pretty hard; he will then jump over not merely the proper distance but a great deal more than is required. He will never need a blow after that, but will jump the minute he sees anybody coming up behind him. When he is used to taking a leap in this way, let the rider mount and put him first at small and then at larger ditches, pricking him with the spur [44] just as he is about to leap. Prick him with the spur in the same way in teaching him to leap up and to leap down. If the horse uses his whole body at once for all these, it will be much safer for him and for his rider than if his quarters are not well gathered in as he leaps or jumps up or down.

Going down hill must be taught him at first on soft ground, and finally, when he gets used to it, he will like to run down much more than to run up. As for the fears that some folks feel of dislocating the horse's shoulders in riding down hill, they should take courage from the knowledge that the horses of the Persians and Odrysians,[45] all of whom habitually run their races down hill, are not a bit less sound than Greek horses.

I shall not omit to tell how the rider himself ought to conform to all these movements. When the horse bolts suddenly off, the rider should lean forward, for then the horse would be less likely to draw in under the rider and jolt him up; but he should bend back when the horse is being brought to a poise, as he would then be less jolted. In leaping a ditch or running up hill, it is not a bad thing to lay hold of the mane,[46] so that the horse may not be troubled by the bit and the ground at the same time. Going down a steep place, the rider should throw himself well back, and support the horse by the bit, so that rider and horse may not be carried headlong down the hill.

It is well that the rides should be in different directions occasionally, and that they should be sometimes long and sometimes

short.   The horse is apt to dislike [47] this
less than riding always in the same places
and over the same distance.   The rider
must have a firm seat when going at full
speed over all sorts of ground, and must also
be able to use his weapons well on horseback.   Hence there is nothing to be said
against the practice of riding in the hunt,
where there is a suitable country with wild
animals; [48] but where these are not to be had,
it is good training for two riders to arrange
together, one to fly from the other on horseback over all sorts of ground, wheeling about
with his spear and retreating again, while the
other pursues with buttons on his javelins
and on his spear.   Whenever he gets within
javelin-shot, he is to hurl his button-tipped
javelins at the runner, and to strike him with
his spear when he overtakes him within striking distance.   If they come to close quarters,
it is well for one to pull his adversary towards
him and then to thrust him back all of a sudden; this is the way to unhorse him.   But
the proper thing for the man who is being
pulled to do, is to urge his horse forward;
for by so doing, he will be more likely to

unhorse the other man than to get a fall
himself.

And if ever there is cavalry skirmishing,
when two armies are set in array against each
other, and the one side pursues even to the
enemy's main body, while the other retreats
among its friends, it is well just here to bear
in mind that while one is among his friends
he is both brave and safe in wheeling among
the first and pressing on at full speed, but
that when he gets near the foe he should
keep his horse well in hand; for thus, while
doing hurt to the enemy, he could probably
best escape being hurt by them himself.

The gods have bestowed upon man the gift
of teaching his brother man what he ought to
do by word of mouth; but it is evident that
by word of mouth you can teach a horse
nothing. If, however, you reward him with
kindness after he has done as you wish, and
punish him when he disobeys, he will be most
likely to learn to obey as he ought. This
rule, to be sure, may be expressed in a few
words, but it holds good in every branch of
the art of horsemanship. For instance, he
would receive the bit the more readily if

some good should come of it every time he received it; and he will leap and jump up and obey in all the rest if he looks forward to a season of rest on finishing what he has been directed to do.

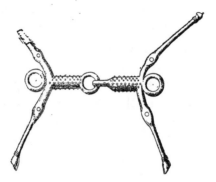

CHAPTER IX.

S O far, then, it has been stated how a person would be least likely to be cheated
in buying a colt or a horse, and least likely
to spoil him in use, but particularly how one
could produce a horse with all the qualities
that a rider needs in war. Now, on the
chance that you should happen to have a
horse that is either too high-mettled for the
occasion or too sluggish, this is perhaps the

proper time to set down how to treat either
one in the most correct fashion.   In the first
place you are to know that mettle is to a
horse what temper is to a man.   Exactly,
therefore, as a man who neither says nor does
anything harsh would be least likely to rouse
the temper of his neighbour, so one who
avoids fretting a high-mettled horse would be
the last to exasperate him.   At the very out-
set, then, in mounting, care should be taken to
mount without annoying him.   After mounting, the rider should sit quiet more than the
ordinary time, and then move him forward
by the most gentle signs possible.   Next,
beginning very slowly, induce him in turn to
quicker paces in such a way that the horse
may reach full speed almost without knowing it.   Every abrupt sign that you make
him — sudden sights, sounds, or impressions
— all disturb a high-mettled horse just as
they do a man.   [Abruptness, you must remember, always confuses a horse.[49]]   If you
want to collect a high-mettled horse when he
is dashing along faster than is convenient,
you should not draw rein abruptly, but
should win him over gently with the bit,

calming him down and not forcing him to be still. Long stretches, rather than frequent turns, calm horses down, and leisurely riding for a good while soothes, calms down, and does not rouse the spirit of the horse of mettle. But if anybody expects to calm such a horse down by tiring him out with riding swiftly and far, his supposition is just the reverse of the truth; these are exactly the circumstances in which the high-mettled horse tries to carry the day by main force, and in his wrath, like an angry man, he often does much irreparable harm to himself and his rider. A high-mettled horse must be kept from dashing on at full speed, and utterly prevented from racing with another; for, as a rule, remember, the most ambitious horses are the highest-mettled.

Smooth bits [50] are more suitable for such horses than rough; but if a rough one is put in, it must be made as easy as the smooth by lightness of hand. It is well also to get into the habit of sitting quiet, especially on a high-mettled horse, and utterly to avoid touching him with any other part than those which we use in securing a firm seat. You must

know that it is orthodox to calm him down
with a chirrup [51] and to rouse him by clucking; still, if from the first you should cluck
when caressing and chirrup when punishing,
the horse would learn to start up at the
chirrup and calm down at a cluck. So when
a shout is raised or a trumpet blown, you
should not let him see you disturbed, least
of all should you do anything to alarm him,
but should quiet him down so far as you can
at such a time, and give him his breakfast
or his dinner if circumstances should permit.
But the best piece of advice I can give is not
to get a very high-mettled horse to use in
war.

As for a sluggish horse, I think it sufficient
to set down that your method of handling
him should at all times be just the opposite
to that which I recommended in the case of
the high-mettled one. [52]

CHAPTER X.

IF you desire to handle a good war-horse
so as to make his action the more magnificent and striking, you must refrain from
pulling at his mouth with the bit as well as
from spurring and whipping him. Most
people think that this is the way to make
him look fine; but they only produce an
effect exactly contrary to what they desire,—
they positively blind their horses by jerking
the mouth up instead of letting them look
forward, and by spurring and striking scare
them into disorder and danger. This is the

way horses behave that are fretted by their
riders into ugly and ungraceful action; but
if you teach your horse to go with a light
hand on the bit, and yet to hold his head
well up and to arch his neck, you will be
making him do just what the animal himself
glories and delights in. A proof that he
really delights in it is that when a horse is
turned loose and runs off to join other horses,
and especially towards mares, then he holds
his head up as high as he can, arches his
neck in the most spirited style, lifts his legs
with free action, and raises his tail. So
when he is induced by a man to assume
all the airs and graces which he puts on
of himself when he is showing off voluntarily,
the result is a horse that likes to be ridden,
that presents a magnificent sight, that looks
alert, that is the observed of all observers.
I shall now attempt to explain how I think
this result may be obtained.

In the first place you must own at least
two bits.[53]   Let one of them be smooth,
with the discs on it good-sized; the other
with the discs heavy, and not standing so
high, but with the *echini* sharp, so that,

when he seizes it, he may drop it from dislike of its roughness. Then, when he shall have received the smooth bit in its turn, he will like its smoothness and do everything on the smooth bit which he has been trained to do on the rough. He may, however, come not to mind its smoothness and to bear hard upon it; and this is why we put the large discs on the smooth bit, to make him keep his jaws apart and drop the bit. You can make the rough bit anything you like by holding it lightly or drawing it tight.

No matter what the kind of bit, it must always be flexible. When a horse seizes a stiff bit, he holds the whole of it at once against his bars; he lifts it all, just as a man does a spit, at whatever point he takes it up. But the other kind acts like a chain; only the part that you are grasping remains unbending, and the rest hangs loose. So, as the horse is always after the part that is getting away from him in his mouth, he drops the bit from his bars. For the same reason little rings are hung from the joints of the bit in the middle, so that the horse, in trying to catch them with his tongue and teeth, may

not think of snatching up the bit against his
bars.[54]

I will set down the definitions of flexible
and stiff bits, in case some reader may not
know them. The bit is flexible when the
joints are broad and smooth where they meet,
so that it bends easily; and all the pieces put
on round the joints are more likely to be
flexible if they are roomy and not tight. On
the contrary, if the different parts of the bit
do not run and play into each other easily,
the bit is a stiff one.

Whatever the kind of bit, it must be used
according to the following rules, which are
in every case the same, provided that it is
desired to give a horse the look that has been
described. The horse's mouth must not be
checked too harshly, so that he will toss his
head, nor too gently for him to feel it. The
moment he acknowledges it and begins to
raise his neck, give him the bit. And in
everything else, as I have insisted over and
over again, the horse should be rewarded
as long as he behaves well. When you see a
horse show his pleasure by carrying his neck
high and yielding to the hand, there is no

need of using harsh measures, as though you were forcing him to work; he should rather be coaxed on, as when you wish him to rest. He will then go forward most cheerfully to his swift paces. A proof that the horse enjoys fast running is that when he has got loose he never moves at a walk, but runs. It is his nature to enjoy it, unless he is obliged to run an excessive distance. Neither horse nor man likes anything in the world that is excessive.

When it comes to his riding in a proud and stately style, — in the first part of his training we accustomed him, you remember, to dash forward at full speed after making the turns. Well, after he has learned this, if you support him by the bit and at the same moment give him one of the signs to dash forward, the bit holds him in and the signal to advance rouses him up. He will then throw out his chest and raise his legs rather high, and furiously though not flexibly; for horses do not use their legs very flexibly when they are being hurt. Now if, when his fire is thus kindled, you let him have the bit, the slackness of it makes him think that he is

given his head, and in his joy thereat he will
bound along with proud gait and prancing
legs, imitating exactly the airs that he puts
on before other horses. Everybody that sees
such a horse cries out that he is free, willing,
fit to ride, high-mettled, brilliant, and at once
beautiful and fiery in appearance.

So much for this subject, in case you are
an admirer of such action.

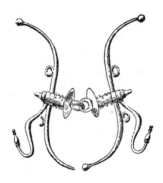

CHAPTER XI.

IF you chance to wish to own a horse for parade,[55] a high-stepper and of showy action, such qualities are not, as a rule, to be found in every horse, but he must have, to start with, the natural gifts of high spirit and strong body. Some people fancy that if a horse has supple legs, it follows that he will be able to rear his body on them; but this is not the fact. It is the horse with supple loins, and short and strong ones too, that can do this. I do not mean the loins at the tail, but at the belly, between the ribs and

the haunches.   Such a horse will be able to
gather the hind legs well in under the fore.[56]
Now when he has gathered them well in, if
you take him up with the bit, he falls back
on his hocks and raises his forehand so that
his belly and sheath can be seen from the
front. You must give him the bit when he
does this, and it will look to the spectators
as if he were doing all of his own accord
the prettiest feat that a horse can do.   There
are, to be sure, some persons who teach this
movement either by tapping the hocks with
a rod, or by directing somebody to run along
by the side and strike him with a stick under
the gaskins. But for my part, I think, as
I have said all along, that it is the best of
lessons if the horse gets a season of repose
whenever he has behaved to his rider's
satisfaction.

For what the horse does under compulsion,
as Simon also observes, is done without
understanding; and there is no beauty in it
either, any more than if one should whip and
spur a dancer. There would be a great deal
more ungracefulness than beauty in either a
horse or a man that was so treated. No, he

should show off all his finest and most brilliant performances willingly and at a mere sign. If he goes on at his exercise till he is covered with sweat, and then if you dismount and unbridle him the moment he rears up in fine style, you must be sure that he will come to the act of rearing with a will. This is the attitude in which the horses of gods and heroes are always depicted, and men who can handle a horse gracefully in it are a magnificent sight. The horse rearing thus is such a thing of wonder as to fix the eyes of all beholders, young or old. Nobody, I assure you, either leaves him or gets tired of watching him as long as he presents the brilliant spectacle.

Yet if it chance that the owner of such a horse should command a troop [57] or regiment of cavalry, he should not aspire to be the only brilliant figure himself, but should try all the more to make the whole line that follows a sight worth seeing. If he goes on ahead at an extremely slow pace, with his horse rearing very high and very often, it is obvious that the rest of the horses would have to follow him at a walk. What could there be at all brilliant in such a sight as this? But if you rouse your horse and take the lead at a gait neither too fast nor too slow, but simply suited to the horses that are most spirited, alert, and graceful in action, with such leading the general effect is complete, and the horses prance and snort all together, so that not only you yourself but all that follow after would be a sight well worth seeing.[58]

To conclude, if a man buys his horses skilfully, feeds them so that they can bear fatigue, and handles them properly in training them for war, in exercising them for the parade and in actual service in the field, what is there to prevent him from making his horses more valuable than when he acquired them, and hence from owning horses that are famous and from becoming famous himself in the art of horsemanship? Nothing except the interposition of some divinity.

CHAPTER XII.

I WISH also to set down how the man who
is to run the hazard of battle on horseback should be armed. To begin with the
cuirass.[59] This must always be made to fit
the body; for if it fits well, the body supports its weight, but if it is very loose, the
shoulders have to carry it all by themselves.
As for too tight a cuirass, it is a strait-
jacket and not a piece of armour. Next,
as the neck is one of the vital parts, I say
that a covering should be made for it rising
out of the cuirass itself to fit the neck.[60]
This will at once be an ornament; and if it
is made as it should be, it will cover the

rider's face when he pleases as far as the nose. For a helmet the Boeotian [61] is the best, in my opinion, since it most completely protects all the parts that are above the cuirass, without preventing you from seeing. Let the cuirass be made so as not to hinder sitting nor stooping. Round the belly, the groin, and thereabouts, there should be flaps of such material and number as to protect these parts. Since the horseman is disabled if anything happens to his left arm, I consequently recommend the newly invented piece of armour called *the arm*.[62] It protects the shoulder, the arm, the elbow, and the part that holds the reins, and it can be extended or bent together; besides it covers the gap left by the cuirass under the armpit.

The right arm must of course be raised whenever the rider wants to hurl his javelin or to strike a blow. The part of the cuirass that hinders this must therefore be removed, and in its place flaps put on at the joints, unfolding all together when the arm is raised and closing when it is lowered. For the arm itself, something worn like a greave [63] seems to me better than to have it of a piece with

the cuirass. The part of the arm that is
bared when it is raised [64] must be protected
near the cuirass with calfskin or bronze, else
it will be left unguarded in its most vital part.

Now, as the rider himself is in extreme
danger if anything happens to his horse, the
animal also should be armed with a front-
let, breastplate, and thigh-pieces; [65] the last
serve at the same time to cover the thighs
of the rider. Above all, the horse's belly
should be protected, as being the most vital
and the weakest part. It may be protected
with the cloth. This cloth [66] must also be of
such material and so sewed together as to
give the rider a safe seat and not to gall the
horse's back. For the rest, this should be
the armour for horse and man; but as the
shins and feet would of course project below
the thigh-pieces, they too may be armed
with top-boots [67] of the leather of which shoes
are made. These will at once protect the
shins and cover the feet.

This and the grace of the gods is the defen-
sive armour. For offensive, I recommend the
sabre [68] rather than the sword; for the rider
being aloft, a scimitar blow will be more in

place than the thrust of a sword. Instead of a spear of scantling, which is weak and clumsy to carry, I am inclined to recommend two javelins[69] made of cornel wood. A skilful person can throw one and then use the other in front, on the flank, or in the rear. They are also stronger than the spear and handier to carry.

I recommend hurling the javelin at the longest possible range. This gives more time to recover oneself and to seize the other javelin. I will set down in a few words the best method of hurling the javelin. Throw forward the left, draw back the right, rise from the thighs, and let it go with the point slightly raised. Then it will carry with the greatest force and the longest range, and it will be sure to hit the mark, provided the point is always aimed at the mark when you let it go.

This completes the hints, lessons, and exercises on which I was to write for the private. The knowledge and practice necessary for the commander of cavalry have been set forth already in a different work.[70]

THE GREEK RIDING-HORSE.

XENOPHON'S "Treatise on Horsemanship" is the oldest extant work on the
subject in any language, and the only one
which has come down to us in either Greek
or Latin. That the author was well entitled
to begin it as he does, will be granted by
every reader of his masterpiece, the Anabasis. But though in the ill-fated expedition
which that book describes, he travelled
nearly three thousand miles, generally on
horseback, yet this journey occupied only a
little more than a year of his life; and prob-

ably before the expedition, and certainly after it, he saw service in the cavalry.

We know very little of the life of Xenophon before the year 401 B. C., in which he joined the army of Cyrus. He was an Athenian, and from a very early age was the follower and friend of Socrates. Whether at the time of the Anabasis he was forty years old or only a little over thirty, is a question which not all the wisdom of the learned has yet been able to settle. After the disastrous failure of Cyrus's enterprise, it was Xenophon, until then a mere honorary staff-officer, who aroused his companions from their dejection; the remainder of the Anabasis tells the story how his courage and skill brought them back to Greek lands from among the Persians. But his success was not appreciated at Athens, and he was banished for serving with Spartans and against the Persians, with whom the Athenians had latterly allied themselves. Becoming again a soldier of fortune, he joined the king of Sparta, Agesilaus, and followed him against Athens and Thebes in the battle of Coronea, 394 B. C. For his services the Spartans presented him with an

estate at Scillus in Elis, about 387 B. C.; and
there he lived for more than fifteen years,
with his wife Philesia and their sons Gryllus
and Diodorus. In this retirement were produced several of his well-known works.
After the battle of Leuctra, in 371, he was
driven out of Scillus and went to Corinth.
Some tell us that the Athenians recalled him
from exile, and that his last years were spent
in his native city; others say that he died in
Corinth. It is certain that his sons, at least,
were in the service of Athens in the campaign which closed with Mantinea in 362.
Not long before this battle he wrote "The
General of Horse," as we know from allusions
in it to the approaching hostilities. This
book, in turn, is referred to in the treatise
on Horsemanship, which must have shortly
followed; and one likes to believe that both
were designed by the old soldier to serve for
the guidance of his sons. The labor of love,
if such it was, failed not of reward. The sons
were worthy of their father, and for their
courage and manly beauty won the title of
the Dioscuri, the "Great Twin Brethren."
The elder, Gryllus, crowned his life by falling

gloriously at Mantinea. "And there came one to Xenophon as he was offering sacrifice, and said, 'Gryllus is dead.' And Xenophon took off the garland that was on his head, but ceased not his sacrifice. Then the messenger said, 'His death was noble.' And Xenophon returned the garland to his head again; and it is in the tale that he shed no tears, but said, 'I knew that I begat him mortal.'" So runs the story; and it is added that Diodorus came safely out of the battle, and lived to rear a son of his brother's name. Xenophon himself died at a good old age, not later than 355.

There is no reason for doubting the tradition that Xenophon's family belonged to the Equestrian * class in the state, and that consequently he served in the cavalry in his youth. He was old enough to have borne a man's part in the last years of the Peloponnesian War and during the episode of the Thirty Tyrants; but history does not even mention his name in connection with either. Still, his whole bearing during the retreat of the Ten Thousand was far from being that of a mere

* See p. 75.

tiro in military affairs, and it is safe to
assume that he had already seen service in
the Athenian cavalry. Even after the battle
of Coronea he still had opportunities for
keeping up his acquaintance with horses.
He was always as far as possible from being
a closet scholar; and no man not a lover
of the free, vigorous outdoor life of the
country could write, as Xenophon does in
the " Oeconomicus," with such a particular
acquaintance with all the various sides of a
country gentleman's life. The preparation
of the soil for all its different products, the
tilling and sowing, and then the reaping,
threshing, and winnowing of the grain, the
planting and tending of trees and flowers,
the care of that all-important olive which
entered into so many of the relations of
Greek life, — all these were familiar to him,
and the oversight of the farm-labourers and
bailiffs as well. Nor did he neglect field-
sports. Once a year there was a grand hunt
on his estate to which all the country round
was invited; and his treatise on Hunting,
with its full account of the breeding and the
training of dogs, shows that the annual hunt

was by no means the only one in which he took part. Surely these pursuits called for horse-raising, horse-training, and horse-riding; and that he became a master in each, the treatise on Horsemanship is evidence enough.

This treatise is confined to the horse that is to be ridden, not driven; and the remarks which follow will therefore be limited in the same way. Riding, as a habit, seems to have come into practice later than driving; at least, this is true of the Greeks. A few passages in Homer are often quoted to show that even in the Heroic Age men sometimes used horses for riding; but this interpretation of the passages is a mistake, and the whole general tone of Epic poetry proves that driving was the common practice.[71] In battle, cavalry was utterly unknown. The heroes fought in chariots, the mass of the army on foot; and journeys, even over mountainous country, were made in chariots.

But in the course of the following centuries there came about a change. We cannot trace its development; but it is a fact that in the Olympic games, in which originally the only equestrian contests were chariot races, there was instituted a race for full-grown riding-horses as early as the thirty-third Olympiad (648 B. C.). In battle the chariot had disappeared even before the Persian wars, but its place was not filled by cavalry until after them. The Athenians had no cavalry at Marathon; and although we know that wealthy citizens kept horses, it is probable that they were bred for racing. Doubtless it was acquaintance with the Persian cavalry that led to the organization of a body of horse at Athens. From the first and throughout its history, it was a *corps d'élite*, selected from the second highest class of citizens in order of wealth. The whole body consisted of only a thousand men, one hundred from each of the ten Attic tribes; each hundred was commanded by a *phylarch*, and the entire corps by two *hipparchs*. It was under the especial oversight of the Senate; entrance into it, while enforced upon the physically and pecuniarily able, was governed by a strict examination, and the horseman was required to present him-

self before an examining committee,* with his
charger, and his equipments, all in a condition
to conform to the law.   In spite of their care,
however, the Greeks never accomplished the
revolution in military art which gave cavalry
a decisive rôle in action.   This was reserved
for the Macedonians.   Greek cavalry was
used, as a rule, only to harass a marching
enemy, or to follow up and complete a victory already won ; and probably horsemen
seldom went nearer than within javelin shot
of a body of infantry in line of battle.

That only the rich could serve in this arm
is evident from the facts that each man had to
supply his own horse, and that horses were
very expensive animals.   A very ordinary
horse cost three minae, or sixty-four dollars ;
a fine animal, such as would be used in war
or for racing, much more.   Thus we hear of
what might be called a thoroughbred as cost-
ing twelve minae,[72] one hundred and eighty-
six dollars.   Xenophon paid a little less than
this for a war-horse which he bought in
Lampsacus.   Such prices for fine horses

* See the accompanying illustration, and its description on page 163.

seem low to us; but it should be remembered
that the cheapness of a given article is rela-
tive to the cost of other articles at the time
in question. In Greek antiquity, the neces-
saries of life were in general to be bought for
comparatively less money than at the present day. A house cost from three to one
hundred and twenty minae ($54 to $2,160),
according to its size, situation, and condition;
perhaps an average price was from ten to
forty minae ($180 to $720). Barley cost
two drachmae the *medimnus* (thirty-six cents
for a bushel and a half); wheat, three
drachmae (fifty-four cents). An ox could be
had for from fifty to one hundred drachmae
(nine to eighteen dollars); a sheep, for ten
to twenty drachmae; a sucking pig, for three
drachmae; a lamb, for ten drachmae. For
the usual garment of the working classes the
same price was paid as for a lamb ($1.80);
for a cloak, such as cavalrymen wore, twelve
drachmae ($2.16). These prices are gleaned
by Boeckh * here and there throughout the
literature. A comparison of them makes it
evident that a horse was an expensive piece

* In " Die Staatshaushaltung der Athener."

of property; and indeed horse-owning, with
all that was too apt to follow it, became a
synonym for extravagance.

Horse-raising was a pursuit for which the
nature of the Greek soil was not well fitted;
the countries were too rugged and mountainous, the plains in them few and small. Chief
among the breeds for beauty, courage, and
endurance was the Thessalian.   It was re-
nowned in the very earliest times, but then
of course for driving and not for riding. The
mares of King Diomedes which ate human
flesh, the horses of Rhesus, of Achilles, and
of Orestes in the race described by Sophocles
in the "Electra,"—finally, to come down from
mythology to history, Alexander's charger,
Bucephalas, were all of this famous breed.
Others in high favour were the Argive,
Acarnanian, Arcadian, and Epidaurian; but
nothing is known of the differences between
these breeds or of the peculiar merits of
each.

In spite of the natural disadvantages of the
soil of Attica, the Athenian young men devoted themselves with much zeal to the raising and training of horses for the turf or for

war; and old Strepsiades * was not the only
father who had to lament that he was ruined
by a horse-complaint. The great space devoted on the frieze of the Parthenon to the
Athenian cavalry shows clearly what a high
estimation was set upon the possession of
beautiful horses, and on dexterity in the man-
agement of them. Instruction in riding
began to form a special branch in the education of the higher classes,† and it was therefore natural that men should begin to write
on the art of horsemanship.

The celebrated rider Simon, of whom more
hereafter, was the earliest writer on this art
whose name is known to us. He was soon
followed by Xenophon. From the latter's
treatise we can discover the point which the
art had reached in the first half of the fourth
century before the Christian era. We learn
from it that the only gaits of the horse were
the walk, the trot, and the gallop with both
leads; that he was trained in leaping as well
as in the demi-pesade, the volte, and the
oblong career with sharp turns at both ends;

* In the comedy of the "Clouds" by Aristophanes.
† See page 169.

that the use of the jointed bit and of the spur
was understood; but that curbs, saddles, and
stirrups were not yet invented. We get also
much information on the nature of the animal himself, and on the care that was taken
of him. I have found it more convenient to
say what seemed necessary on all these matters in the notes which follow this essay.
But Xenophon's first chapter is devoted to
the physique of the animal; and in it he sets
forth what, in his opinion, are the distinguish-
ing marks of a good horse. This is a subject
which may be better treated here than in the
notes.

In the matter of judging the points of a
horse, the ancient requirements were not in
all respects like the modern. The advance
in anatomical knowledge accounts for some
differences; but it is also probable, as Schlieben * observes, that we, like the men of old,
are prejudiced by habit in favour of the type
with which we are familiar. If qualities
which they thought beautiful seem ugly to
us, it should be remembered that our standard does not always conform even to that of
the last century.

* In " Die Pferde des Altertums."

Our knowledge of the taste of the Greeks in this matter is drawn from two sources, — the literary and the artistic. Schlieben, in his interesting book on the Horse in Antiquity, seems to think that the three principal forms of art — vase-paintings, reliefs, and statues in the round — each exhibit peculiarities of treatment innate to the artistic form, which make it impossible to reach, from a comparison of them all, any distinct conception of the best type of Greek horse. Then turning to the writers, he is further confused by finding that points of excellence upon which they all agree are not apparent in the works of the artists. Hence he assumes different ideals for the artists and the writers. He even thinks that in one point, at least, the unanimous agreement of the writers is reversed by as complete a contrary agreement in works of art. This point is the mane. He makes the common errors of believing that all the artists represent it as short, and that all the writers say that it should be long. Neither belief is more than an assumption, and a baseless one at that, as will appear later. The fact is, Schlieben seems to expect to find in the works of all sorts of artists, good, bad, and indifferent, the same consensus that really is to be found in the writings of the authors. But the works of art have survived to us from different centuries by means of all kinds of accidents, and they were produced for all kinds of reasons. The books have survived, generally, for the reason that they were fittest for survival. The authors lived, none of them, before the classical period, and each of them undertook to describe a horse because he knew the animal himself, and had spent a good part of his life with horses, or because he could copy the words of authors of more practical experience than his own. There can be no question of the vast advantage of the books over the works of art in deciding such a matter as this.

There would be nothing very surprising, therefore, in the want of agreement in art, if such want there be, upon a type of horse which we can take for the ideal animal. But nobody should thence proceed to argue that there was no such type already determined by judges of horseflesh and agreed upon even by artists. It would be much more

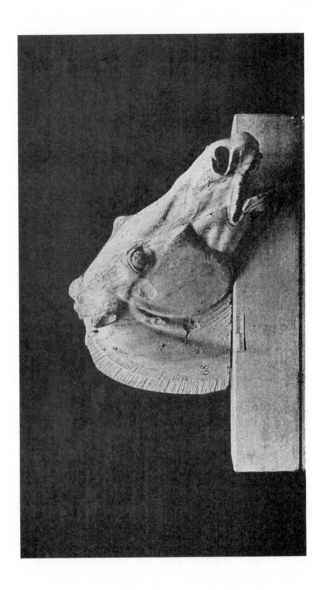

likely that it was the want of technical skill
which prevented the artist from representing
what he had in mind to represent; then, too,
he might be fettered by convention. When
we look at a picture on an archaic vase, we
are standing at the very cradle of the art of
painting, — in order of time the last of the fine
arts which the Greeks developed. And we
see on vases of the more cultivated period
many things which illustrate the power which
lies in methods sanctified by custom — that is,
in convention — to over-ride the real knowledge of the art of painting and the greater
perfection of technique which existed at the
time of the production of such works.   In
criticising an equestrian statue or a relief for
a frieze, one should always remember that it
was intended to be placed at a considerable
elevation and to be looked at from below, so
that exaggeration of certain parts was often
necessary, — such, for instance, as in the
treatment of the eyes of the famous horse's
head by Phidias * in the eastern pediment of
the Parthenon. But when all allowances are
made, a perfect horse is as rare a thing in

* See the opposite cut.

Greek art as he is in nature. Even on the
Parthenon frieze, where there are finer horses
than in any other works of Greek art, some
animals have faults which are apparent to the
veriest tiro.   In fact, if we should judge
altogether by what has survived to us, it
must be admitted that in representing the
horse in all the different forms of art the
ancients have been surpassed by modern
artists. By Phidias we have only the heads
that were in the pediments; for the figures
on the frieze, although designed by him,
were certainly not carved by his own hand.
But Phidias stood alone, and far above contemporaries and successors.   Still, in spite of
the fact that many ancient representations of
the horse have no claim to beauty or to cor-
rectness in composition, there are others
which will better bear criticism, some de-
serve high praise, and we read of artists
who won great fame in antiquity for the
realism with which they depicted the animal.
Apelles, to whom Philip and Alexander often
sat for their likenesses, is said to have painted
a horse [73] with such truth to nature that a
live horse neighed at the picture !   Pauson

was commissioned to paint a horse rolling,* but he painted him running with a cloud of dust about him. The man who gave the order naturally objected, whereupon the master turned the picture upside down, and behold! the patron's stipulations were fulfilled.[74] Criticism could discover only one defect in a painting by Micon; the famous rider Simon remarked that he had never before seen a horse with eyelashes on the lower lids.[75] Such stories, in spite of manifest exaggerations, show that extant works are not a fair criterion of the skill of the great painters. Not a single work remains that can be traced to any of them; but doubtless to their art, in comparison with what survives, might have been applied lines like Donne's, written of a contemporary of his own, —

> "A hand or eye
> By Hilyarde drawne, is worth an history
> By a worse painter made."

In sculpture, both in the round and in relief, and in reliefs on coins, the extant works are far more satisfactory; for they rep-

* See p. 131.

resent branches of art which had reached
near to perfection before the Greeks really
began to develop painting.   But here again,
as I have said, we lack complete examples of
works illustrating the horse by the greatest
masters, except perhaps by the best designers for the coinage.   On the whole, it seems
impossible, from a comparison of the works
of art alone, to determine what shape of
horse was generally approved by the Greek
connoisseur.   It remains to inquire whether
the literature helps us in this direction.

The oldest known description in Greek of
a good horse was contained in Simon's treatise on Horsemanship, of which we have only
fragments.   One, however, is of considerable
length, and this happens to contain his advice
on the choice of a horse.   Then comes
Xenophon; but after him we find nothing
professing exactness until the Roman period.
Varro, writing in 37 B. C., and Vergil, who
published his "Georgics" a little later, are
the only others before the Christian era.
Then come in the first century Calpurnius
and Columella, in the third Oppian and
Nemesian, and in the fourth Apsyrtus, Pela-

gonius, and Palladius.[76]   There are of course
countless allusions to the points of the horse
in numerous other authors, but I have here
named all the extant writers who have described with any exactness and completeness
the best type of the animal; and in another
part of this book (p. 107) will be found
translations which I have made from them
all.

These writers are scattered through a period
of nearly eight hundred years, but it is evident that they all had in mind an animal of
the same general stamp.   Schlieben writes as
though the descriptions given by the several
writers really differed in essential particulars;
but this is very far from being the case, and
his study of the passages cannot have been
exact.   Xenophon's description is by all odds
the most complete; in his first chapter he
touches upon over thirty points, many more
than are mentioned by any other writer.   A
careful examination of them all shows that
there are only five points mentioned by
others but omitted by him; namely, shoulder-
blades (large, Simon and Apsyrtus; broad,
Varro; strong, Nemesian); teeth (small,

Simon); gaskins (not fleshy, Simon); veins
(visible all over the body, Varro); coronet,
(moderate, Pelagonius). On the other hand,
the other writers never disagree with Xenophon in the points which they do mention.
The only approach to such disagreement
is the long barrel apparently required by
both Simon and by Palladius; but Xenophon was speaking only of riding-horses,
while there is nothing to show that these
writers had not also in mind horses for driving. It is true that we find some additions
to Xenophon's descriptions of certain points;
but these are only additions and not contra-
dictions, and he would doubtless have agreed
with most of them. Such, for instance, are
the muscles bulging out all over the chest
(Vergil, Columella, Apsyrtus, Palladius), the
jaw brought close to the neck (Simon,
Oppian), the straight cannons (Columella,
Oppian). It appears, then, that there is a
very close agreement among the different
writers; further, the resemblance in their
language and the order in which they take
up the various points show that they were
frequently copying from one another or from

a common source now lost to us.* There can
be little doubt, therefore, that even before
Xenophon's time an ideal or normal type
had been established which was to find
acceptance throughout the whole period of
Greek and Roman antiquity.

Now, when we compare Xenophon's description of a good horse with the best
horses on the frieze of the Parthenon, we find
a remarkable similarity. In fact, as "Stonehenge" † remarks, " here we have described
a cobby but spirited and corky horse, with a
light and somewhat peculiar carriage of the
head and neck, just as we see represented on
the Elgin marbles." It has been thought by
some that Xenophon based his description
upon these very reliefs, and it is of course
possible that they may have served as a sort
of guide to his words. But from earlier
works still, in vase-paintings of extremely

* A lost work by the elder Pliny contained a description of the normal horse, generally accepted by
his contemporaries. See his Natural History, viii,
162.

† In his book on the Horse, near the beginning of
which he gives the most exact translation of Xenophon's description which I have ever seen.

rude workmanship, presenting pictures which
to the Philistine are nothing but ridiculous
caricatures, — even in these early productions
and still more frequently on the later vases,
there are traces which show that it was the
artist's hand that was at fault, or that he was
governed by convention, and that there was
present before his mind something very like
the conception which the assistants of Phidias
were enabled to work out, — some of them,
it is true, without the full measure of success,
others almost to perfection.   It was, I believe,
not the want of a type, but of the genius to
give expression to the type, or again it was
the power of convention, that prevented those
artists whose works have survived from
enabling us to settle from their productions
the question which has engaged us.   The
type of horse portrayed on the frieze was a
very old one, even in the fifth century; the
minute description of the points given by
Xenophon and confirmed by other writers,
helps us to detect the faults which a Greek
horseman would have seen in some of the
figures on the frieze.   To obtain, therefore,
a correct conception of the Greek idea of a

good horse, one should compare the first
chapter of Xenophon's treatise with the best
animals on the Parthenon.   Some assistance
may be had from the brief summary of the
defects of a horse as given by Pollux * (1,191).
These are as follows : —

" Horn thin, hoofs full, fat, soft, flat, or, as
Xenophon calls them, low-lying.   Heavy
fetlocks, varicose veins in the shanks, flabby
thighs, hollow shoulder-blades, projecting
neck, mane bald, narrow chest, head fat and
heavy, large ears, nostrils converging, sunken
eyes, thin meagre sides, sharp backbone,
rough haunches, thin buttocks, stiff legs,
knees hard to bend."

There is one point, however, which seems
to call for special notice, and that is the
mane.   As I have already said, Schlieben
has fallen into the common error of believing
that the writers require the mane to be long,
but that in works of art it is nearly always
cut short.   But a careful reading of the
authors will show that the word " long " is
never applied to the mane by any of them.
The adjectives are " thick," " full," " fine-

* See note 76.

haired," " crinkly," and it is said to fold over
to the right. All these expressions might be
applied to a short, and the first even to a
hogged, mane. Xenophon comes nearest to
calling the mane long when he uses the
phrase ἕως ἂν κομῶσιν, which I have rendered " while it is flowing" (chap. v, p. 32).
But the context shows that it is there a
question of mane or no mane, not of short or
long. And there is nothing in the chapter
to show that Xenophon disapproved of keeping the mane down by trimming; there must
be plenty to take hold of in mounting, he
says, and enough for beauty. On the other
hand, it is evident that he would have had no
hogging of the mane, and none of the other
writers mention such a thing. But Xenophon's
very insistence on the beauty of a flowing
mane seems to me to show that not all the
world agreed with him; he is as earnest
about it as if he were a member of the
Humane Society preaching against docking.
It is not surprising to me, therefore, to find
in works of art the portrayal of a different
fashion. Probably most people, if asked to
describe the mane of the Greek horse, would

say that it was hogged; at least, that is the
answer which I have almost invariably received on putting the question. There can
be, I think, no doubt that the hogged mane
was a fashion which existed in Greek antiquity, silent about it though the writers may
be; the difficulty is to discover whether it
always existed side by side with the flowing
mane, or whether it went out of fashion after
a certain period. Still harder would it be to
determine whether hogging was practised
only upon horses of a certain breed or size,
as it generally is with us, or upon horses intended only for special purposes. Into these
questions I have not entered, but I believe
light might be cast upon them by a careful
study and comparison of works of art.[77] A
mere glance through such a well-known book
as Baumeister's "Denkmäler des Klassischen
Altertums" shows a number of examples of
hogged manes. Omitting for the moment
the Parthenon marbles, striking instances will
be found as follows: the Oropus relief, p. 69;
Phigalia frieze, plate xliv; very ancient
terra cotta from Melos, p. 1290; Dipylon
vase, p. 1943; Mycene vase, p. 1941; black-

figured vase, p. 2081. But it would be a great mistake to suppose that the hogged mane is the only fashion in art. In the same book examples of long straight or long curly manes are found as follows: black-figured vases, pp. 67, 725; Corinthian vase, p. 1962; * altar of Pergamon, p. 1257; Vienna cameo, p. 1390; François vase, plate lxxiv; Trajan's column, p. 2057. Short and curly manes are to be seen; for instance, on a late vase, p. 728, and a Pompeian wall-painting, p. 667. It is a dangerous thing to offer an opinion on such a point without much more exhaustive research than I have made; but I have been led to believe, from these and many pictures in other books, that the hogged mane was an old fashion, which in the time of Xenophon was passing away.[78] Although I admit that much is to be said on the other side, yet I am strengthened in this belief by observing that out of nearly a hundred horses on the Parthenon friezes only about thirty have hogged manes, and that frequently these thirty have an unfinished look in other points, so that many of them, as works of

* I give an illustration of this vase on page 22.

art, are of inferior quality. It should be said, however, that the manes of the pediment horses are all hogged.

In size, it is clear that the ancient Greek horse was smaller and not so tall as ours. His descendants in their own country still retain this characteristic feature. We might infer from the whole tone of the descriptions by the writers, that they were speaking of a small and compactly built animal, although we find no exact statements of size or height. But there is one passage at the beginning of Xenophon's seventh chapter which is very significant. It appears that an approved method in mounting was to " lay hold of the mane *about the ears*." We should need no further evidence than this to prove that Athenian cavalry horses were much less high than the ordinary saddle-horse is now; but it is supported by the illustrations in art, and especially by the reliefs of cavalry horses on the Parthenon. But just here let me say that I believe that most people fancy the Greek horse a great deal smaller than he really was. This is because they judge him from the Parthenon frieze and other compositions,

such as vase-paintings, in which he appears
side by side with men standing on the ground.
The unthinking observer, comparing the
height of the horses with the height of the
men in the same composition, and finding
that the men are usually as tall or even
taller than the horses, concludes that the
Greek horse must have been a very small
animal indeed.   But such a conclusion is
made in ignorance or in neglect of an important principle of Greek art.   By this it was
required that in a composition of numerous
figures the heads of all should be nearly
upon a level, whether the men were walking,
riding, or driving.   This principle, called
Isokelismos, does not in practice offend the
eye, which, recognizing the effect of the
whole as a work of art, is not troubled by
the exactness of levels, untruthful to nature
though it may be.   But of course it utterly
forbids us to use the apparent height of the
men in such a composition as any standard
for the real height of animals.   A better
means of judging from the frieze is by observing how far the feet of the riders hang
down below the bellies of their horses.   The

distance appears to be much greater than in
the case of men on horseback to-day. It
should be remembered, however, that the
cella frieze was placed more than thirty-five
feet above the floor of the temple, and that
the outer row of columns prevented the spec-
tator from standing at a distance to examine
the frieze. He had to look almost straight
up. In the British Museum, as well as in
others, the slabs or casts of them are placed
much lower. But in their original position,
the perspective would prevent the feet of
the men from seeming to dangle so far below the bellies of their horses.* The dif-
erence, however, would be slight, and the
whole build of the horse in these as well as
in other works of art, stamps him as a small
animal. Of course the size and height of
horses varied then just as now. The differ-

* Since I wrote the above, my friend **Dr.** Hayley
informs me that he heard Professor Kekulé make the
same remark in a course of lectures on the frieze.
Professor Kekulé also observed that the sculptors of
this frieze had anticipated some of the discoveries
made by instantaneous photography in the positions
of the horse in motion.

ent breeds may have had their distinctions
in this respect; but, as I have said, we know
nothing of them.   It may be significant, however, that on Thessalian and Macedonian
coins the riding-horses often appear equal
in size to our own.   Little, if anything, can
be inferred from the almost giraffe-like proportions of the animal on the most archaic
vases.

From the physique of the horse I pass to
his nature.   In reading Xenophon's treatise
one may be struck by the frequency with
which this man, well used to riding as he
was, refers to the horse as a dangerous animal to come near.   While it should be
remembered that the Greeks generally used
entire horses, not geldings, for all purposes
and especially for war, yet this will not wholly
account for Xenophon's constant tone of caution; and it is probable that the process of
domestication, extending through centuries,
has made a very great difference in the tem-
perament of the animal, as we know it, from
what it was in the classical period.   Ancient
literature is not without its stories [79] of the
devotion of the horse to his master; but even

in these the wildness or the savageness of
the animal is generally brought out, showing
itself often in a bloody revenge taken by the
steed upon the warrior who has killed his
rider, or in absolute refusal on the part of
the horse to be mounted by any save his
accustomed rider. There is, in fact, nothing
to show that the Greek ever made a friend
of his horse, least of all that there was ever
between them that beautiful relation which
is so common between horse and man in
Arabian tales. Even the poets, from Homer
down, did not appreciate what might be
made of it. Witness the answer of Achilles
to his horse Xanthus when the noble animal
did his best to warn his master: " Xanthus,
why prophesiest thou my death? Nowise
behooveth it thee;" and he puts him off
with scarcely less harshness than that of
Balaam to his ass.[80] Xenophon probably
comes as near to loving the horse as any
Greek ever did, and no modern humanitarian
was ever more earnest in urging over and
over again the principle of treating horses
with kindness. His precept, "Never deal
with the horse when you are in a passion,"

is a whole treatise in itself.   But he has not a single word of love for the horse any-where, and does not even suggest that the rider should try to win his horse's affection for its own sake.   All his teaching is practi-cal: be kind to your horse and he will do as you desire.   The explanation of all this may be that to the Greeks the horse sug-gested war, with all the merciless qualities which characterized it in antiquity.   They kept no riding-horses in our sense of the word, and we never read of a Greek as taking a ride for pleasure.   Their horses were bred and reared primarily to be machines of battle, or for the scarcely less fiercely contested struggles in the hippodrome.   They had but a slight place in the every-day life of men; to be sure, they were sometimes used on journeys, especially over mountains; but even ambassadors generally travelled on foot, and carriages were usually drawn by mules.   The pomps and processions on festive days were so contrived as to be part of the horse's training for war.   His real business lay among warriors; for he was like the horse in Job that "saith among the trumpets, Ha, ha; and he smelleth the battle afar off, the thunder of the captains and the shouting." *

It may be appropriate, then, to finish this sketch by setting down what is known of the famous charger of Alexander the Great. The names and characteristics of many horses of gods or heroes have been transmitted to us; but Bucephalas is the only horse belonging to a mortal about which the Greeks have left any particular description.[81]   He was of the best Thessalian breed, black, with a white star, and very large.   As Gellius says, " Et capite et nomine Bucephalas fuit."   The fact is that, long before this famous animal, a well-known type of Thessalian horses had given rise to the name, which means " Bull-head." [82]   This type had small ears set well apart, thus leaving the brow wide and the poll large.   " Some people," says an unknown writer in the " Geoponics," " reckon among the finest horses those with eyes which are not a match; such, they say,

---

* Cf. Vergil, Georgics, III, 83 : —

Tum siqua sonum procul arma dedere,
Stare loco nescit, micat auribus et tremit artus,
Collectumque premens volvit sub naribus ignem.

was Bucephalas." If this story is true, he had what is sometimes called a "China eye." King Philip bought him from one Philoneicus, a Thessalian, — for thirteen talents, as Plutarch says; for sixteen, according to Pliny (from thirteen to eighteen thousand dollars). Either price is probably an absurd exaggeration, the result of the later reputation of the animal. Evidently the king was not a believer in Xenophon's principle of giving a horse a thorough trial before buying him; for, says Plutarch, when they brought the king's new purchase into the place where they were to try him, it appeared that he was a fierce and unmanageable beast. "He would neither allow anybody to mount him, nor obey any of Philip's attendants, but reared and plunged against them all, so that the king in a rage bade them take him away for an utterly wild and unbroken brute. But Alexander, who was by, cried out, 'What a fine horse that is which they are spoiling! The clumsy cowards, they can't handle him.' Philip said nothing to this at first; but when his son kept on grumbling, and seemed to be in a great taking, he said at last, 'Are you find-

ing fault with your elders because you know
any more yourself, or can handle a horse
any better than they?'   'I could handle
that horse, at any rate, a great deal better
than anybody else,' was the answer.   'And
what will you forfeit for your rashness if you
fail?'   'The price of the horse, by Zeus!'
There was a burst of laughter, and it was so
agreed.   In a moment Alexander ran up to
the horse, seized the reins, and turned him
to face the sun; for it seems that he had
observed that what frightened the creature
was the sight of his own shadow playing to
and fro on the ground before him.   After a
little patting and coaxing, seeing him full of
courage and spirit, Alexander quietly slipped
off his cloak, and springing up bestrode him
unharmed.   Feeling the bit gently with the
reins, he restrained him, without whipping
or hurting him, until he saw that the horse
had given up all threatening behavior, and
was only hot for the course; then he let
him go, and urged him on by raising his
voice and using his heel.   The attendants
of Philip were anxious and silent at first; but
when he turned and came back full of just

pride and pleasure, they all raised a cheer,
except his father. But he, they say, wept
for joy; and after Alexander had dismounted,
said, 'You must go look for a kingdom to
match you, my son; Macedonia is not large
enough for you.'"

Alexander was only a boy of twelve when
this happened; for it was before Aristotle
became his tutor, — an event which took
place when the prince was thirteen. Bucephalas, however, was no young colt, but
fourteen years old even then. Ever after,
though he would allow the groom to ride
him bareback, yet when his trappings were
on he suffered none save Alexander to mount
him; others who tried it met with the same
savage behavior which he had shown at his
first trial, and were forced to take to their
own heels to save themselves from his. But
he bent his knees when Alexander appeared,
so as to make mounting easy, without wait-
ing for the word of command. For the rest
of his life he was Alexander's favorite charger,
and went with the great king on his expedition to the East. In Hyrcania he was stolen,
but was returned in a hurry on proclamation

that unless he was brought back the whole
nation — men, women, and children — should
be cut off. "Thus," remarks Arrian, "he
was as dear to Alexander as Alexander was
terrible to the barbarians." He carried the
king in all his great victories, and finally
died at the age of thirty * from wounds received in the battle against the Indian king
Porus in 327 B. C. Alexander, says Gellius,
had pressed recklessly forward into the very
ranks of the enemy, and was the mark for
every spear. More than one was buried in
the neck and flanks of the horse; but though
at the point of death, and almost drained of
blood, he turned, carried the king with a
bold dash from the very midst of the foe,
and then and there fell down, breathing his
last tranquilly now that his master was
safe, and as comforted by it as if he had
had the feelings of a human being. No
wonder that Alexander founded the city
of Bucephalia in his honor, and grieved
for him as if he had lost a friend; no
wonder that of this horse only in all Greek

---

* The usual extreme limit, according to Aristotle,
of a horse's years. See page 127.

literature is it written that he was dear to his master.

It is generally believed that the fine bronze found at Herculaneum * is a reduced copy of the figures of Alexander and Bucephalas from the famous group which was made by Lysippus, at Alexander's own order, to represent a scene at the battle of Granicus. Of another likeness of Bucephalas we have only a well-known anecdote. Alexander once went to see his own portrait with that of his horse, painted by Apelles. The king did not praise the picture as it deserved. But his horse, on being brought up, neighed at the horse in the picture as if it were a real animal; whereupon, "Your Majesty," said Apelles, "your horse seems to be a good deal better judge of painting than you are."

* See cut on page 69.

POINTS OF THE HORSE.

THE following are the descriptions of a good horse, according to the ten Greek and Roman writers referred to on page 86.

SIMON.

On Simon and his work, see page 119. I have translated from the text of Blass, " Liber Miscellaneus editus a Societate Philologica Bonnensi," 1863,

p. 49 ff. The fragment here translated is all that
remains of Simon's book on the horse, except a few
quotations from it in Pollux.

IF one desires to know this subject well,
it seems to me that the shape of the horse
is the first thing. To begin with the country
of birth, you must know that, so far as Greece
is concerned, Thessaly is the best. As to
size there are three accepted terms, — large,
small, and good-sized, or, if you like, moderate; and it is obvious which size each of the
terms will fit. But moderate size is best in
every animal. I cannot tell a good horse
from his colour; however, it seems to me
that a mane which is of the same colour
throughout and of fine hair is generally the
best, and besides it is most unlike that of
the ass and the mule. A point second to
none in consideration is that the horse must
be short above and long below, so that the
distance shall be short from the withers to
the haunches, but as long as possible from
the hind legs to the fore; next, that he must
be sound-footed. A good hoof for a horse
is the light and handy sort, neither broad
nor too high, and having little flesh but

thick horn.   The sound is also a sign of
the good hoof; for the hollow sort has
more of the cymbal ring than the full and
fleshy.   Let him have supple pasterns and no
stiffness of the fetlock joints; his shanks
should be shaggy, with the parts about the
back sinew and the shank sinewy and with
as little flesh as possible up to the knee.
Above, however, the leg should be fleshier
and stouter.   Let the space between the
two legs be as wide as possible, for then
he can throw out his legs without interfering.   His chest should be neither too
narrow nor too broad, and his shoulder-
blade very large and very broad indeed.
Let the neck be slender near the jaw, supple,
flattened back to the rear, but bending down
to the front from the slenderest part.   The
head should be advanced, and the neck not
short.   Let him have a high poll, and a
head flat-nosed but light; the nostrils should
be very large, the jaws slender and a match
for each other, the eyes large, very prominent and bright, the ears and teeth small, the
jaw as small as possible, and the part between
the neck and the jaw very slender.   The

withers and seat should be very large, the
sides very broad and deep, and the loin
supple (you can tell that the loin is supple if he does not stand on both his hind
legs at the same time, but is constantly
changing from one to the other), the haunch
very large and broad, the flank very small.
The gaskins should not be very fleshy; and
he should have small stones. Between the
hams he should not be prominent nor full,
but only rather swelling a little, and the
breech should be very small and well out of
sight. Let him hold his tail high, and have
it thick at the base and long. This for the
shape of the horse. He is by far the best that
has all these points; and second is he that has
the majority of them, including those which
are of the most service. The colt begins to
be driven two years after birth. About this
time he sheds his first teeth, when he is
thirty months old; the second a year after,
the last in another year or in less time; and
he is at his prime for swiftness and courage
at six years old.

VARRO.

This extract is taken from the "Res Rusticae,"
2, 7, 5. The book was written in 37 B. C., when the
author was eighty years of age. The translation is
made from the Latin text of Keil.

WHAT the horse is to be like can be guessed
from the colt, if it has a small head with well-
marked parts, black eyes, nostrils not narrow,
ears close to the head; mane thick, dark,
rather crinkly, and of fine hair, folding over
to the right side of the neck; broad, full
chest; large withers, moderate-sized belly,
flanks drawn in as you go down, broad
shoulder-blades, tail full and crinkly; shanks
stout, matching, shaped off somewhat towards
the inside; knees round and not large, hoofs
hard. The veins should be visible all over
the body, convenient for treatment when he
is not well.

VERGIL.

From the "Georgics," 3, 79 ff., published about
29 B. C. Translated from the text of Ribbeck.

LOFTY is his neck and brisk-moving his
head; short in the barrel is he, plump of
back, his undaunted breast swelling with
folds of muscle. The bays and grays are

noble beasts; the poorest colour is white and yellow. Then, when arms clash afar, he cannot keep the spot, but pricks up his ears, quivers in every limb, and clouds roll from his fiery nostrils. His thick mane on his right shoulder falls, and there it lies; his chine is double where it runs along the back, and his firm-horned hoof rings loudly as he paws the ground to hollows.

CALPURNIUS SICULUS.

From the "Eclogues," 6, 52 ff., written probably between 57 and 60 A D. Translated from the Latin by E. J. L. Scott.

My beast displays
A deep-set back; a head and neck
That tossing proudly feel no check
From over-bulk; feet fashioned slight,
Thin flanks, and brow of massive height;
While in its narrow horny sheath
A well-turned hoof is bound beneath.

COLUMELLA.

From "De Re Rustica," 6, 29, 2 ff., written a little before 65 A. D. Translated from the Greek text of Schneider.

SMALL head, black eyes, nostrils flaring, short ears set up straight; neck supple and

broad without being long; mane thick and
hanging down on the right side; broad chest
with the muscles bulging out everywhere;
large straight shoulders; sides curving, seat
double, belly drawn in, stones small and
alike, broad flanks sinking in; tail long,
thick, and crinkly; shanks supple, deep, and
straight; knee well-turned, small, and not
turned in; rounded buttocks; thighs bulging
with muscles everywhere; hoofs hard, high,
hollow, and round, topping off with moderate-
sized coronets.

OPPIAN.

From the "Cynegetica," 1, 176 ff., a poem written
in the first part of the third century. Translated from
the Greek text of Schneider.

LET him be large himself and round of
limb, but small be the head he raises high and
loftily above his neck; lofty his crest, but let
the jaw come down low, inclining towards the
throat; broad and beautiful should be his
front between the brows, and from above let
thickly clustering locks fall about his face;
under the brow his bright eyes flash with
ruddy fiery light; wide are his nostrils,

small his ears, and fair-sized his mouth; his
neck well rounded, shaggy with the mane,
like the helmet with its nodding flowing
crest; wide his chest, the barrel long, back
broad, chine double, and loins plump; his
long-haired tail should flow out far behind
him; his thighs should be well-knit and
muscular; below, his shank bones should
be straight and long, round, handsome, free
from flesh, like the long-antlered stag's whose
feet are storm-swift; his pasterns sloping,
his round hoofs coming well up above the
ground, compact, horny, and strong.

NEMESIAN.

From the " Cynegetica," verse 245 ff., written in
the second half of the third century. Translated from
the Latin text of Haupt.

HIS back is smooth and broad of surface;
flank very long; the belly small, even on large
animals; brow lofty, ears mobile, head handsome, and crest high; eyes flashing with
radiant light; his neck mighty and arching
back to his stout shoulders; the breath of his
hot nostrils rolls forth like steam; his foot

loves not the task of standing still, but his hoof smites the ground continually, and his high spirit wearies out his own limbs.

APSYRTUS.

Apsyrtus was a veterinary surgeon under Constantine the Great in the first part of the fourth century. The translation is from the compilation called the "Geoponics," 16, 1, 9 ff.

SMALL head, black eyes, nostrils not converging, ears erect, neck supple; mane thick, somewhat crinkly, and falling on the right side of the neck; chest broad and muscular, shoulders large, forearms straight, belly well-rounded, stones small; seat preferably double, otherwise not humped; tail large and crinkly-haired, shanks straight, thighs muscular; hoof of a good contour, and equally solid on all sides; frog small, horn hard.

PELAGONIUS.

Pelagonius lived in the last half of the fourth century. The translation is from the new edition of his "Ars Veterinaria," § 2, by M. Ihm, Leipzig, 1892.

SMALL head, black eyes, nostrils open, ears short and pricked up; neck flexible and broad

without being long; mane thick and falling on
the right side; broad and muscular chest,
big straight shoulders, muscles sticking out
all over the body, sides sloping in, double
back, small belly, stones small and alike,
flanks broad and drawn in; tail long and not
bristly, for this is ugly; legs straight; knee
round, small, and not turned in; buttocks
and thighs full and muscular; hoofs black,
high, and hollow, topping off with moderate-
sized coronets. He should in general be so
formed as to be large, high, well set up, of
an active look, and round-barrelled in the
proportion proper to his length.

PALLADIUS.

From the "De Re Rustica," 4, 13, 2 ff., written
probably about the middle of the fourth century.
Translated from the Latin text of Schneider.

IN a stallion four things are to be tested, —
his shape, colour, action, and beauty. For
shape we shall try for a large compact body,
height to suit his strength, a very long flank,
big round haunches, breast broad, the surface
of the body all closely knotted with muscles;
foot dry and firm, the horn which forms its

shoe hollow and pretty high. The points of
beauty are a small dry head, with scarcely
anything but mere skin on its bones; ears
short and mobile, large eyes, wide nostrils,
neck erect, mane thick, tail even fuller, hoofs
set on firm and round. In action, let him be
high-spirited, swift-footed, quivering-limbed
(a proof of courage), and willing to be
put to speed from a dead halt and to stop in
the midst of a fast dash without making
trouble. The principal colours are chestnut,
golden, albino, bay, brown, fawn, yellowish,
checkered, dead white, piebald, glistening
white, black, dark. Of less value and of
various degrees of beauty, black mixed with
albino or chestnut, gray with any other colour
you like; dappled, spotted, mouse-colour, or
even duskier. But in the case of stallions,
let us pick out a single distinct colour; others
are to be disdained unless great merit in
other ways makes up for defect in colour.
The same points must be considered in
brood mares; especially they should have
long large barrels and bodies.

NOTES.

1. (Page 13.) Simon was an Athenian, but we do not know exactly when he lived and wrote. The story of his criticism of Micon's picture (see p. 85) sets the earliest limit (Micon was a contemporary of Polygnotus, who was in Athens about 460 B.C.), and Xenophon's mention of him the latest. Various theories have been propounded, such as W. Helbig's, who thought (A. Z. 1861, p. 180) that he was the Simon mentioned in Aristophanes (Knights, 242), and that he was Hipparch in 424 B.C.; and Gerhard's, who recognized him in the figure of a charioteer inscribed with his name on a vase (Auserlesene Vasenbilder, iv, taf. 249). But the earliest known Greek prose which has survived is the tract on the Athenian State, written between 424 and 413 B.C.; and the fragment of Simon's work (see p. 107) bears no evidence of

being older, and is probably not so old. It is
likely that it was written at the beginning of the
fourth century. Xenophon, in speaking of Simon,
scarcely uses the tone which would have been
proper in speaking of a very ancient writer.
Besides the long fragment a few short ones are
preserved in Pollux. According to Pliny (Nat.
Hist. 34, 76), a statue of Simon dressed as a
knight was made by Demetrius (who flourished
probably in the latter half of the fifth century) ;
but this may be only a mistaken allusion to the
statue of the horse mentioned by Xenophon. It
is supposed by Ernst Curtius (Die Stadtgeschichte
von Athen, p. 188), who calls Simon a contemporary of Pericles, that this statue was intended
to embody a perfect representation of the ideal
horse, just as the famous work by Polycleitus illustrated the proportions of the ideal man ; but this
is of course a mere theory, unsupported by literary
evidence.

2. (PAGE 13.) The Eleusinion, in Athens, was
a precinct of Demeter, Kore, and Triptolemus,
with two temples ; it often served as the goal of
processions, especially cavalry displays.

3. (PAGE 14.) This excellent advice stamps Xenophon at once as a true horseman. Horace,
though he was no rider, knew the doctrine too ;
witness Sat. 1, 2, 86 : —

" Regibus hic mos est, ubi equos mercantur : opertos
Inspiciunt, ne si facies, ut saepe, decora
Molli fulta pede est, emptorem inducat hiantem
Quod pulchrae clunes, breve quod caput, ardua cervix·
Hoc illi recte ; "

which may be rendered, —

Swells, when they buy horses, have a way of cov·
ering them up when they look them over, for fear that
a handsome shape set upon tender feet, as often happens, may take in the buyer as he hangs open-mouthed
over fine haunches, small head, and stately neck.
And they 're right in it.

4. (PAGE 14.) Throughout this book it should
be remembered that the ancients did not shoe
their horses. The Romans, indeed, used for
mules the *solea*, a sort of sock of leather completely covering the hoof and tied about the
fetlock, strengthened underneath by a plate of
iron (Catullus, 17, 26). Nero substituted plates
of silver (Suetonius, Nero, 30), and his luxurious
wife, Poppaea, gold (Pliny, Nat. Hist. 33, 140).
But we do not hear of socks for horses, except
that in the retreat of the Ten Thousand an Arme-
nian showed the Greeks how to wrap their horses'
feet in little bags when travelling through deep
snow. But of course all this is quite different from
the modern practice of permanent shoeing. This
latter is first mentioned in literature in the time
of the Emperor Justinian, the first half of the
sixth century (Martin, Les Cavaliers Athéniens,

p. 400) ; but shoes were probably known earlier.
It is said that one was found in the tomb of King
Childeric, who died in 460 A. D.   There is a cut of
it, taken from Montfaucon, in Ginzrot, ii, tab.
86, 1.   The cut makes it practically identical with
the modern shoe ; but Beckmann, in his " History
of Inventions," justly doubts the trustworthiness
of the picture.

5. (PAGE 15.) The Greek word used by Xenophon is χελιδών, which literally means " swallow ; "
and the frog was so named from its resemblance
to the forked tail of the bird.   In later Greek we
find it called βάτραχος, " frog " (Geoponics, 16, 1,
9, from Apsyrtus), and in Latin *ranula*, " little
frog " (Vegetius, 1, 56, 31).   The French call it
fourchette ; the Germans *Strahl*. It will be observed
that Xenophon's principle (supported by the other
writers) of keeping the frog well up from the
ground, and calling for a high and hollow hoof is
not always accepted in modern times.

6. (PAGE 15.) This remark, and many of the
works of art show that it was not the custom to
trim down the fetlocks.   In warm climates they do
not grow very long, and instead of disfiguring the
foot serve rather to set off its contour.

7. (PAGE 16.) The Greek word is περόνη, which
has given much trouble to translators and commentators.   It means literally the pin of a brooch,

— the Greek brooch being shaped somewhat like the modern safety-pin. In the anatomical writers it was naturally applied to the small bone in the man's arm or leg, — the radius or fibula. In the horse, of course, this bone is above what we call his " knee ; " and Xenophon, who has not yet reached this knee, cannot be thinking of a part above it. Hence it has generally been believed that he meant a bone in the knee itself, one of the astragals. But I believe that Xenophon was not thinking of the skeleton, but rather of the animal as he looked in the flesh. Indeed he may not have understood the anatomy of the horse in its relation to man's ; certainly below he speaks of the forearm as if it corresponded to the upper instead of to the lower arm in man. What, then, was more natural than that he should compare the back sinew to the small bone of man's leg ? This granted, he has described what naturally follows when a horse with " gummy " legs (just what he has been speaking of) is put to hard work. He breaks down, or gives way in the back sinews. This explanation seems to have occurred to none of the commentators, — not even to Dindorf, though he had the advantage of using the fragment of Simon (see p. 109) in which the word περόνη is used exactly as in Xenophon. I am happy to be supported in my view of the passage by Dr. Lyman, Dean of the Harvard Veterinary

School, to whom I submitted my opinion. After reaching it, I found that the same translation of the word was used by Stonehenge (see p. 89).

8. (PAGE 16.) I have used the word " forearms " for greater clearness. Xenophon calls them thighs (μηροί), applying the same word to the fore as later to the hind legs. No special horse dialect had yet developed; but the same words, so far as possible, were used of horses as of men.

9. (PAGE 16.) The lean, dry head with small bones, was esteemed the most beautiful; and this point is insisted upon by all the ancient writers except Nemesian, who says merely that the head should be handsome.

10. (PAGE 17.) Xenophon seems to mean the " bars " here. Their fineness was a thing not to be seen by the eye, but to be discovered by trial in riding, as he says in the third chapter, in his remark about the Volte.

11. (PAGE 17.) The reason for this requirement, so well recognized for race-horses, is well stated by Professor Flower in his admirable little book called " The Horse : a Study in Natural History " (p. 142, American edition): " Owing to the great length of the soft palate and its relation to the upper end of the windpipe, breathing takes place entirely through the nose. When men, dogs, and many other animals, in consequence of any great exertion, begin

to pant and require an additional quantity of air to
that which is ordinarily taken in by the nose, the
mouth comes to the aid of that channel and is
widely opened; but the horse under the same
circumstances can only expand the margins of the
nostrils, for which action there is a very efficient
set of muscles, acting on the cartilaginous framework which supports them and determines their
peculiar outline."

12. (PAGE 17.) Small ears, set well apart so
as to leave a large poll, formed the type of
beauty which gave rise to the name Bucephalus
(βουκέφαλος, "bull-" or "ox-headed"). This was
applied to a valuable breed of Thessalian horses
(Aristophanes, Frag. 135) long before it was
given, in a slightly modified form, to Bucephalas,
the famous charger of Alexander. Examples of
this type are the bronze head in the Uffizi and
the famous marble head by Phidias (see frontispiece and plate facing p. 83).

13. (PAGE 17.) The idea is that in well-built
horses, in good condition, the flesh rises on each
side of the spine so that the latter does not stick
up like a ridge but lies in a slight depression.
This quality was of course even more highly appreciated before the days of saddles than it is now.
It is mentioned also by Vergil, Columella, Oppian,
and Apsyrtus.

14. (PAGE 18.) The word used here, ὑπόβασις, is very vague, and has given rise to various interpretations. I think it refers to the act of gathering in the hind legs in doing the demi-pesade, described in the eleventh chapter.

15. (PAGE 18.) This fact is noted also by Aristotle (Part. Anim. 4, 10, 12) and Pliny (Nat. Hist. 11, 260), who state that young quadrupeds can reach their heads to scratch them with the hind feet; Pliny adds that they cannot graze without bending the forelegs. Buffon independently observed these facts. Schlieben (p. 86) gives two Arabian methods of estimating what will be the height of horses. By the first a cord is stretched from the nostril over the ears and down along the neck; this distance is compared with that from the withers to the foot; the colt will grow as much taller as the first distance exceeds the second. By the other method, the distance between the knee and the withers is compared with that from the knee to the coronet; if it has reached the proportion of two to one, the horse will grow no taller.

16. (PAGE 20.) See p. 75.

17. (PAGE 23.) By the word "markers," γνώμονες, Xenophon means the milk-teeth, and he is therefore advising against the purchase of a horse over five years old. The times of the shedding of these teeth were well understood by the ancients, as we know from Aristotle, Hist. Anim. 6, 22, 12; Varro, Res Rusticae, 2, 7, 2; Apsyrtus in the "Geoponics," 16, 1, 12. What we now call the "marks" are of course in the permanent teeth; they are spoken of by Varro, Ibid. 2, 7, 2; Columella, 6, 29, 4; Apsyrtus, Ibid. 16, 1, 12. Aristotle sets the average age of horses at from eighteen to twenty years; some, he says, live to be twenty-five or thirty; and with great care a horse may live to be fifty, though thirty is generally the highest limit (Hist. Anim. 6, 22, 8).

18. (PAGE 24.) The word here and in chapter seven is πέδη, which properly means "fetter." Godfrey Hermann, in his essay on the words which the Greeks used to denote the gaits of the horse (Comment. Lips. p. 59), has shown that the Volte is meant in these passages.

19. (PAGE 24.) He seems to mean that if, for example, the stable lies to the right, the horse will throw his head to the left, and advancing his right shoulder, will make a bolt for it. The left rein being loose and the right side of the mouth hard, the rider will have no control over the animal. But the passage is obscurely worded, and has been variously interpreted. It may mean "unless they are hard-mouthed and also are directed towards home."

20. (PAGE 27.) The stable was part of the town-house, and was situated on one side of the front door. In the country it may have been an out-building.

21. (PAGE 27.) Aristotle (Oeconomica, 1, 6, 4) tells of a Persian who was asked, "What is the best thing to make a horse plump?" and who answered, "His master's eye."

22. (PAGE 28.) Barley was the ordinary feed for Greek horses. Apsyrtus says that the disease was an indigestion coming from eating when out of breath after a journey or a run. Among the symptoms he mentions that the horse is doubled up, cannot bend his legs, and refuses to move, throws himself down, and takes his food lying. A like account is given by Vegetius (Mulomedicina, 5, 43, 1). Aristotle calls the disease incurable "unless it cures itself" (H. A. 8, 24, 4).

Besides barley, Greek horses were frequently fed on spelt, sometimes on hay; and wheat is mentioned two or three times by Homer. A mash of barley and green herbs was prescribed in cases when a mash would now be given.

23. (PAGE 28.) Courier tried the experiment, and describes it as follows: "À Bari, ville maritime de la Pouille pierreuse, on garnit le sol d'une écurie construite pour quatre chevaux, d'un lit de cailloux pris sur la plage, et arrondis par la

mer, dont les plus gros pouvaient avoir le volume
d'un boulet de quatre. Ce lit, de dix-huit pouces
à peu près de hauteur sous la mangeoire, qui fut
exhaussée d'autant, s'abaissait en pente vers le
mur opposé. Trois chevaux y furent placés pieds
nus : l'un, poulain de quatre ans, race des envi-
rons de Cirignola, qui n'avait jamais en de fers ;
l'autre, de huit ans, d'Acquaviva, ferré ordinaire-
ment de devant ; le troisième, vieux cheval de
troupe. De ces trois chevaux, le premier seule-
ment avait le sabot bien fait et la corne assez
bonne. On les pansait à l'écurie, d'ou ils ne
sortaient que pour la promenade ; on mettait sous
eux la nuit, au lieu de litière, quelques brins de
sarment. Leur urine tombant à travers les pierres
sur le pavé très-uni de l'écurie, s'écoulait à l'ordi-
naire avec l'eau qu'on y jetait de temps en temps
pour nettoyer la place ; de sorte que le cheval
était toujours à sec. Chaque jour, soir et matin,
le poulain trottait plusieurs reprises à la longe, sur
la grève, ou l'on avait amassé des cailloux pareils
à ceux de l'écurie. Au bout de deux mois et
demi, sa corne était plus compacte, et la fourchette
surtout avait acquis une solidité remarquable. Il
fit le voyage de Bari à Tarente passant par
Monopoli, Ostuni, Brindisi, Lecce, Manduria, tous
chemins de traverse remplis de pierres, et revint
sans être ferré ni incommodé : à la vérité on ne
l'avait monté que deux jours ; mais il aurait résisté

à de plus grandes fatigues, et il était aisé de voir que les mêmes soins continués l'auraient mis en état de se passer de fers toute sa vie ; il fut vendu.   Les deux autres n'eurent pas le même succès : leur corne, gâtee par les clous, se fendait et s'exfoliait pour peu qu'ils marchassent ; mais peutêtre qu'avec le temps ils se seraient fait un bon pied.

" Cette épreuve eut lieu dans les mois juillet, août et septembre ; on ne peut douter qu'elle n'eut complètement réussi sur des chevaux calabrais, qui ont meilleur pied que ceux de la Pouille."

Stalls paved as Xenophon describes are not by any means unknown both here and in England. The late E. F. Bowditch, Esq., of Framingham, was a strong believer in them, though he would by no means have approved the hollow hoof described in Xenophon's first chapter.   But of course his horses were shod, and so shod that the frog and heel were very close to the ground. His object in using the cobble-stones was to stimulate the growth of those parts, and to keep them soft so as to prevent the frog from shrivelling. This softness of the frog and its contact with the ground, he thought, prevented all jar on the foot, the frog acting as a buffer.

24. (PAGE 29.) The Greek cared for his body by bathing and rubbing as well as by the free use of oil. Hence Pollux (1, 201) advises rubbing the horse's bars with the fingers to make them fine, and washing the mouth and lips with warm water and anointing them with oil.

25. (PAGE 31.) The muzzle was of thin bronze, perforated like a sieve, or of bronze wire or wicker. See cut, p. 34.

26. (PAGE 31.) It was the custom among the Greeks and Romans to give the horse a roll in fine sand after he had exercised. So Pheidippides in the "Clouds" of Aristophanes (32), after a dream of horse-racing, calls out in his sleep to his slave to give the horse a roll and take him home. And Isomachus in Xenophon's "Oecono·micus" (11, 18) has his slave do the same thing after his morning's ride. This Isomachus was a fine type of the Athenian of the best period, — pure-minded, honourable, and upright. He was a lover of the country and a fearless rider; and the following account which he gives Socrates of the way in which he was wont to spend his mornings makes a delightful picture. The translation here given was made by Gentien Hervet in 1532. I copy from the edition of 1537 (Thomas Berthelet, printer, London).

"I ryse in the mornynge out of my bed so yerly, that if I wold speke with any mā, I shall be sure to fynde him yet within. And if I haue

any thynge ado in the citie, I go about it, &
take it for a walke. And if I haue no matter of
great importance to do within the cityc, my page
bryngeth my horse afore in to the fieldes, and so
I take the way to my groũd for a walke, better
parauenture, than if I dyd walke in the galeries
and walking places of the citie. And whan I
come to my grounde, and if my tenantes be eyther
settynge of trees, or tyllyng or renewyng the
grounde, or sowynge, or caryenge of the fruite, I
beholde howe euerye thynge is done, and caste in
my mynde, how I might do it better. And after-
warde for the moste parte, I gette me a horsebacke
and ride as nere as I can, as though I were in
warre constrayned to do the same, wherefore I do
not spare nother croked wayes, nor noo shroude
goinges up, no ditches, waters, hedges, nor
trenches, takynge hede for al that, as nere as can
be possible, that in this doing, I do not maime
my horse. And whã I haue thus doone, the page
leadethe the horse trottynge home agayne, and
caryeth home with him into the citie, out of the
cõtre that that we haue nede of. And so than I
get me home againe, somtimes walkyng, and
sometime runnynge. Than I wasshe my handes,
and so go to dyner good Soc. the which is or-
deyned betwene bothe, soo that I abyde all the
daye nother voyde nor yet to ful."

Besides the charm of its language, this transla-

tion is very accurate; there is in it but one real
error, for Xenophon does not say that the page
leads the horse "trotting" home, but that he
"gives him a roll" and then leads him home.

27. (PAGE 31.) Pollux (1, 185) mentions several. The σπάθη, which he describes as wooden
and shaped like a feather, was used for cleaning the
hair. The word really means "any broad blade;"
and this implement is doubtless to be recognized
on an Assyrian relief from Nimroud, representing
the stable of Assurnazirpal. Other implements
were the ψήκτρα, for combing out, of iron with
teeth like a saw, corresponding to our curry-comb;
and the σωρακίς, which seems to have been a sort
of mitten of purple cloth, used by the groom in
rubbing down and to give a gloss to the coat.

28. (PAGE 32.) This prescription goes back to
Homer, Il. 23, 280, "a charioteer . . . who on
their manes full often poured smooth oil, when he
had washed them with water." The Scholiast on
these lines says : " This is why Xenophon recommends the washing of the head and forelock with
water ; " and he adds the irrelevant but interesting
information that about a sixth of a pint of oil was
enough to supple a man's whole body.

29. (PAGE 32.) Upon this passage Berenger
(The History and Art of Horsemanship, by

Richard Berenger, Gentleman of the Horse to
His Majesty: London, 1771) has the following
interesting note (Vol. I, p. 239) : —

" These observations are so true and just that one
could almost think it needless to dwell upon them ;
yet such is the cruelty and absurdity of our notions
and customs in 'cropping,' as it is called, the ears
of our horses, 'docking' and 'nicking' their tails,
that we every day fly in the face of reason, nature, and
humanity. Nor are the present race of men in this
island alone to be charged with this folly, almost unbecoming the ignorance and cruelty of savages ; but
their *forefathers*, several centuries ago, were charged
and reprehended by a public canon for this absurd
and barbarous practice ; however, we need but look
into the streets and roads to be convinced that
their descendants have not degenerated from them;
although his present Majesty, in his wisdom and
humanity, has endeavoured to reclaim them, by issu-
ing an order that the horses which serve in his troops
should remain as nature designed them:
' Who never made her work for man to mend.'— DRYDEN."

" The title of the canon is, —

" 19. *Ut reliquias rituum paganorum quisque
abjiciat.*

*Equos vestros turpi consuetudine detruncatis, nares
finditis, aures copulatis, verum etiam et surdas
redditis, caudas amputatis; et quin illos illaesos
habere potestis, hoc nolentes cunctis odibiles redditis.
Equos etiam plerique in vobis comedunt, quod nullus
Christianorum in Orientalibus facit; quod etiam
evitate.*

" From the influence of a vile and unbecoming custom, you deform and mutilate your horses, you slit their nostrils, tie their ears together, and by so doing make them deaf; besides this you cut off their tails; and when you enjoy them uninjured and perfect, you chose rather to maim and blemish them, so as to make them odious and disgustful objects to all who see them. Numbers of you likewise are accustomed to eat your horses, — a practice of which no Christians in the East were ever guilty. This also you are hereby admonished to renounce entirely."

This canon was number nineteen among those passed at the Council of Calcuith, held in 787 or 785 A. D. It may be found in Spelman's Councils of England, I, p. 293.

30. (PAGE 32.) Aristotle, Aelian, Plutarch, and Pliny all repeat this strange story. Sophocles evidently knew it; I translate from a fragment (598) of his " Tyro " : —

> For my lost locks I mourn, like some young mare
> That rustic drivers catch and hale away
> To where their rude hands in the stables reap
> The golden harvest clean from off her neck.
> They drag her to the mead; in its clear streams
> Mirrored the semblance of her form she sees,
> Her mane with that foul cropping shorn away.
> Oh, then e'en pitiless might pity her,
> Cowering with shame and like to some mad thing,
> Mourning and weeping for the mane that's gone.

On the mane in general, see p. 91 ff.

31. (PAGE 35.) Xenophon says "left;" the Greeks had no technical terms like our "near" and "off."

32. (PAGE 36.) The strap which goes over the crest back of the ears.

33. (PAGE 36.) The word used by Xenophon means properly "net." It is applied to the whole upper part of the bridle with its different straps. The cheek-straps, the headpiece, with the straps running from this, beside the ears, to the front, and often joining a strap which ran down the middle of the face, all formed a sort of network.

34. (PAGE 36.) When a leading-rein or halter was attached to the bridle (see note 38), this caution would not be necessary; for such a rein was fastened to the nose-band or chin-strap, and hence, if it had any pull at all on the jaws, it pulled on both alike. Xenophon means that in the absence of such a halter *both* the bridle-reins must be grasped at once.

35. (PAGE 37.) By this method the helper took the foot or knee of the rider in his hand, and so raised him. It is recommended for the elder men in the cavalry by Xenophon in his treatise on the "General of Horse," 1, 17. It was the privilege of Tiribazus, Satrap of Armenia, when he was at court, to mount the King of Persia in this fashion

(Xen. Anab. 4, 4, 4). A special attendant for this purpose is said to have accompanied Alexander in his battles (Arrian, Anab. 1, 15, 8). At the court of Philip, pages, sons of noblemen, performed this duty for the king (Ibid. 4, 13, 1). Slaves, however, seem to have "made a back;" and the Roman Emperor Valerian, when prisoner to Sapor, was obliged by that haughty prince to mount him in this degrading fashion, and not to offer his hand (Lactantius, "De mortibus persecutorum," 5).

36. (PAGE 37.) By a very neat touch, Xenophon fancies himself on the horse's back, speaking to him encouragingly.

37. (PAGE 38.) Stirrups were unknown till long after the Christian era began. Other methods of mounting are described in the next chapter; but here we see that horses were sometimes taught to stoop or settle down so as to make it easier for the rider to reach his place. This was done in two ways: (1) by bending the knees, and thus lowering the shoulders; (2) by throwing the fore feet forward and the hind feet back, thus lowering the seat, as horses sometimes do naturally when tired. The second is the method here spoken of by Xenophon, who applies to it the word ὑποβιβάζεσθαι. Pollux (1, 213) describes it by saying that in it the horse set his legs apart,

settled in, and lowered himself. A rider about to
mount by this method is represented on the frieze
of the Parthenon, and on a vase from Nola (see
cut on p. 39). That it was employed sometimes
by Roman soldiers is evident from a relief in
Clarac, Musée des Sculptures, Plate 221. But it is
not referred to elsewhere in Greek literature.
Courier had seen this method in use in Germany,
and Jacobs says that it was introduced thither
from England (!) and called *Strecken*. Alexander's horse Bucephalas was taught the first method,
— that of bending the knees (Curtius, 6, 5, 18).
This method is represented on a black-figured
vase in the Hermitage collection (see cut on
p. 30). The Greek word in this case is ὀκλάζειν.

38. (PAGE 39.) From this it appears that a
strap or cord, entirely distinct from the reins, was
attached to the bridle, doubtless to be used in
leading as well as in mounting. (See note 34.) It
may be seen in the cuts on pp. 34, 39, and 29, in
which it is attached to the chin-strap. On a vase-
painting in Gerhard (Auserlesene Vasenbilder, iv,
293, 294, 1) it is attached to the nose-band. A
leading-rein just like the Greek is to be seen in
Assyrian reliefs.

39. (PAGE 39.) As Greek bits had no branches,
the chin-strap was not the equivalent of our curb-
chain, and no leverage came from pulling on it.

It merely kept the bit in place and the mouthpiece from slipping through, and would cause no
pain if pulled down by the halter. The nose-band
was of leather or metal. On the bits, see note 53.

40. (PAGE 39.) The Roman soldier referred to
in note 37 has his hand here. This remark of
Xenophon's throws light on the height of the
Greek cavalry horse. (See p. 95.) Mounting-
blocks were often used. There are several on
the frieze of the Parthenon, and one on the
Gjölbaschi Heroon (Taf. 23, B. 2). They were
placed at convenient intervals along the streets
in Rome by Gaius Gracchus (Plutarch, 7, 2).

41. (PAGE 39.) In this method of mounting,
the spear must have been used much as we use a
vaulting-pole (but of course with only one hand).
It is absurd to suppose that there was a little pro-
jection or crossbar towards the butt of the spear,
which served as a step in mounting. The athletic
Greek would have scorned such a thing. A gem
in the Stosch collection, supposed to represent a
warrior mounting in that fashion, is capable of a
different interpretation; and the spears in Stuart
and Revett (Antiquities of Athens, iii, p. 47) have
nothing on them but the common thong to help
in hurling. Yet the crossbar theory has found
credence with Ginzrot, Berenger, Winckelmann,
Jacobs, Schlieben, and Martin, as well as with all

the commentators on Xenophon's work except Courier, who will have none of it. He describes the way in which the Polish and Austrian lancers of his day, as well as the Cossacks, were in the habit of mounting ; and doubtless this is very like what Xenophon meant : " Ils saisissent de la main gauche les rênes et une poignée de crins, et s'appuyant de la droite sur la pique, un peu penchée vers la croupe du cheval, ils s'enlèvent tout d'un temps, en mettant la pied à l'étrier, et le cavalier se trouve en selle la lance en main."

42. (PAGE 41.) The Greeks had no saddles with trees, nor the Romans until the fourth century, so far as can be judged from works of art. They rode either bareback or upon a cloth which was fastened by a girth under the belly or about the breast of the horse. In works of art the girths are often omitted.

43. (PAGE 42.) This statement seems to be exactly the reverse of the truth ; for the horse in starting to canter turns himself slightly across his line of progress, in order to enable him to lead with that leg which is advanced by this turn. Hence to lead with the left, he turns his head to the right and his croup to the left. Accordingly there has been much discussion of this passage in Xenophon, and various emendations of the text have been proposed by modern editors.   Her-

mann, after various attempts, practically gives the
passage up; and so far no satisfactory explanation
or emendation has been offered. I have endeavoured to translate the Greek exactly as I found
it. If the Greek text is as Xenophon wrote it, I
cheerfully admit that any absurdity in the translation is due to my own misunderstanding of the
Greek rather than to any ignorance on the part
of Xenophon. It should also be observed that
the lead recommended (with the left) is not the
favourite lead to-day.

The walk, trot, and gallop are the only gaits
mentioned in Greek authors. The amble or pace
was certainly unknown to them until after the time
of Aristotle, who says (περὶ ζῴων πορείας, 14) that
if a horse moves the two legs on the same side at
the same time, he must fall. Still it will be observed
that on the Orvieto vase (see cut facing p. 76) the
horses are all moving in this manner. But as
Körte shows (A. Z. 1880, p. 181), this had become the conventionalized manner of representing
the motion of the horse. It is found in Assyrian
and Egyptian art, and from thence passed to the
Phoenician and the archaic Greek, where it is the
regular rule, although some exceptions are found.
It appears on coins down to the best period, and
on red-figured vases of the more severe type. It
was, therefore, not intended to represent a natural
gait in the animal. Pliny (N. H. 8, 166) men-

tions a Spanish breed of horses whose natural gait
was the amble, and adds that this led to the belief
that the trot was in all breeds an acquired gait.

44. (PAGE 46.) The Greek spur had no rowels,
but was merely a small goad fastened to the heel
by straps which passed over the instep and under
the sole. Such spurs have been found in Olympia
and in Magna Graecia, and are represented in
vase-paintings. A book on the development of
the spur, with many beautiful plates, is " Der Sporn
in seiner Formen-entwicklung," Zchille und Forrer,
Berlin, 1891.

45. (PAGE 47.) The Odrysians were a Thracian
tribe, whose power, once extending from the Stry-
mon to Abdera, declined at the end of the fifth
century B. C.

46. (PAGE 47.) This seems at first sight a device
entirely unworthy of a horseman, and Berenger
strongly condemns it; but it is evident, from what
follows, that Xenophon's intention was not to
recommend one to support himself by the mane,
but to prevent the beginner (this book was written
for "the younger of his friends") from disturbing
the horse in his leap by jerking at the bit. The
context shows that it was with the bridle-hand
(thus kept motionless) that the mane was to be
grasped. The expression " it is not a bad thing "
is probably purposely selected; and Xenophon

does not here say, as usual in this book, "it is well." Of course a practised rider would need no such help as the mane to keep his hand quiet. On the frieze of the Parthenon the rider who has his right hand on his horse's head is merely soothing the excited animal (see cut facing p. 89).

47. (PAGE 48.) As Jacobs observes, the rule is a good one, but the reason given for it (and repeated by Pollux, 1, 206) seems to be exactly the reverse of the truth. The horse, as a rule, prefers familiar places, and after constant riding over one road it will be found very difficult to make him go elsewhere.

48. (PAGE 48.) For instance, on Xenophon's estate in Scillus they hunted deer, wild boars, and gazelles; among other animals, hares, bears, and wolves are frequently mentioned as hunted in Greece. The hunt was one of the principal amusements of both Greeks and Romans, as it had been of earlier nations. Much information on the subject will be found in Xenophon's "Cynegeticus," though the work treats chiefly of dogs and hounds, and in the treatise of the same name by Arrian.

49. (PAGE 52.) The words in brackets are, as Cobet pointed out, a stupid interpolation, adding nothing to what has been said already.

50. (PAGE 53.) On the bits see note 53.

51. (PAGE 54.) "Chirrup" is here used, for
want of a better word, to translate ποππυσμός, a
noise made by the lips alone. It is used of a
kiss (Anthologia Palatina, v, 245 and 285), and
therefore does not mean "whistling," as it is generally translated here. The sound is familiar to
every rider, but we use it now to start a horse.
By "clucking," κλωγμός, is meant the sound
made by the tongue against the roof of the
mouth.

52. (PAGE 54.) This advice looks as though
Xenophon were hurried, or as if a lazy horse were
too distasteful a subject for him to treat. He
could not have meant it to be followed to the
letter.

53. (PAGE 56.) There is no evidence for a
curb-chain on a Greek bit, and hence Greek bits
had no leverage. The reins in every case acted
directly on the mouthpiece of the bit. Nor do
we hear of two bits used at the same time, nor of
two sets of reins. In this passage Xenophon
recommends two kinds of bits, — the smooth and
the rough; but it is evident from his language
that these were not the only kinds used in his day.
Here, however, I am concerned only with these
two. What constituted the smoothness of the one
and the roughness of the other? Certainly not

the discs (τροχοί) ; for they were used on both
kinds, and were actually smaller on the rough than
on the smooth.   Evidently, therefore, the difference lay in the nature of the " echini ; " this word,
the plural of " echinus," I have felt it necessary to
transfer from the Greek bodily, for we have none
in English which will exactly express its meaning
here.   The word in Greek, ἐχῖνος, means " sea-
urchin ; "   therefore   the   contrivance   upon   the
mouthpiece of the bit was probably round, and
had on its edges prickly spines, such as we see
on the edges of the sea-urchin's shell.   In the
rough bit these spines were sharp ; Xenophon's
language suggests that there were echini on the
smooth bit, but that their spines in this case were
not sharp.   Fortunately, light is thrown on this
subject by a bit which has actually come down to
us from antiquity.   This bit (see cut, p. 50) was
found on the Acropolis of Athens in 1888, when
the wall and other works of Cimon were in course
of excavation.   It lay among the débris used as
filling at the time of these works.   The bit is
therefore very old, dating back nearly, if not quite,
to the time of the Persian wars, 490 – 479 B. C.   I
take the picture, with part of my description, from
an article by Lechat in the " Bulletin de Cor-
respondance Hellénique," 1890, p. 385.   The
mouthpiece is jointed, and the reins were attached
to the large rings at each end.   What appear to

be branches are not like the branches of our curb-
bits; for they did not serve to support a curb-
chain, nor was a rein attached to them. They
were fastened to the cheek-pieces of the bridle,
and merely kept the mouth-piece in place. Each
cheek-piece divided into two straps, just before
reaching the bit, to which they were attached
at the two small holes in each branch. This
arrangement for attaching the bit was a very old
one; it may be seen on many Assyrian reliefs
(see cut facing p. 145) and on some Greek vases
(see cuts on pp. 20, 23, 27, 39).* See also the
Dodona statuette, p. 44. These pictures show
that the branches lay close against the sides of the
mouth; in the picture of the Acropolis bit (and in
that of the Carapanos bit below) the perspective is
misleading. It is evident that no leverage was
to be had from such branches. We cannot tell
whether the bit which Xenophon had in mind
was attached in this way or not; he himself says
nothing, and such branches are altogether wanting

* On this subject, see an article in the "Revue
Archéologique," 1888, p. 52, where it is shown that a
prehistoric bit found in Switzerland and one found in
the Caucasus region were attached in the same way
as above described. The latter almost exactly resembles the Acropolis bit; the former has no echini,
but is a mere twisted snaffle. In treating the bit, I
do not think it safe to use the illustrations given in
Montfaucon or in Jacobs.

in many works of art. But to return to the
echini. Each part of the mouthpiece of the
Acropolis bit has little spines on it; but these
spines are rounded and not sharp. Further, to
judge from Lechat's description, they rise directly
from the mouthpiece itself, and not from a cylin-
der put on about the mouthpiece. But we know
that the echini were not always actually part of
the mouthpiece; we might infer that they were
not, from Xenophon's remark about "all the
parts put on round the joints;" and this infer-
ence is made certain by the construction of
another ancient bit (cut on p. 60). This bit,
also described by Lechat, is in the Carapanos
collection of bronzes; but unfortunately its country of origin and its age are unknown. Like
the other, it is jointed; but each half of the mouthpiece forms an axis about which play an echinus
and a large disc, the latter being biconvex like a
lens. The spines of the echini are very sharp.
The discs are evidently what Xenophon calls the
τροχοί. But in this bit we have a combination
which he does not recommend; that is, we have
" good-sized " discs, whereas he says that with
sharp echini the discs should be heavy, but not
so high as they are when used on the smooth bits.
It is inconceivable, however, that the discs should
ever have been higher than these. This bit was
attached to the cheek-pieces by the small rings on

the branches; the reins were fastened to the large
hooks which play about the axes of the mouthpiece.   The branches are very large; I know of
only one parallel for them in art, on a vase published in the "Journal of Hellenic Studies," 1890,
plate 2, fig. 6, and possibly on the coin in the cut
on p. 26.

Now, it is clear that neither of these bits corresponds exactly to Xenophon's description.   But
from them I have, I believe, got a clearer idea of
what he meant than is to be had from any of the
commentators on his book.   The horse, we gather
from Xenophon, was to be trained on the rough
bit; hence the discs were low and heavy, probably
like the rollers used on some modern curb-bits.
The sharp echini acted on the "bars" of the
horse if he attempted to seize the bit.   When he
had been taught his lesson, the smooth bit was
substituted.   Here the echini were rounded,
so that they merely suggested punishment without
really inflicting it.   But to prevent him from
getting so used to the smooth bit as not to mind
it, large discs were put on, "to make him keep his
jaws apart and drop the bit."   These discs were
between the bars and the tongue, on each side;
and, these once understood, we see why the horse
is represented with his mouth open in nearly all
Greek works of art.

Xenophon does not recognize a bit consisting of

a single piece of metal (though the Greeks may
have had such bits), but always speaks of one that
is jointed. His expression, "stiff bit," therefore,
applies to one in which the parts — the joints,
discs, and echini — do not play easily about
each other, either from rust, or because the parts
are too tight.

That numerous other kinds of bits, and variations upon these two kinds, were known to the
ancients, is evident from the classical writers, from
Pollux, and from works of art. For example, the
modern roller-bit is found in the mouth of Alexander's horse (cut on p. 69), if one may trust the
large engraving in the "Bronzi di Ercolano," ii,
p. 339. There are also in the Naples Museum
a number of bits, of which I have seen photographs. None of them exactly resemble the bit
described by Xenophon, though several approach
it in details. The whole subject is a good field
for closer investigation, and little confidence can
be placed in the statements found in the ordinary
books on antiquities.

54. (PAGE 58.) The device of hanging little
rings from the middle of the bit is familiar in
modern times.

55. (PAGE 61.) As, for instance, in the Panathenaic festival. The frieze of the Parthenon
represents the parade on this occasion. A com-

ment by Beulé will be found interesting here
(L'Acropole d'Athènes, 2, p. 160) : "La troupe
s'avance au galop, par un mouvement plein
d'ensemble, mais d'une allure retenue et qui n'a
rien d'impétueux. Les chevaux semblent galoper
sur place, ou plutôt se cabrer gracieusement.
Si l'on veut une description du cheval du Parthé-
non, qu'on lise le onzième chapitre du traité
d'equitation. Le type idéal que cherche Xéno-
phon, Phidias l'a constamment copié. La race
thessalienne offre encore aujourd'hui une certaine
ressemblance avec les bas-reliefs de la frise."

56. (PAGE 62.) That is, of course, when the forelegs are raised in the movement described in the
next sentence, the "demi-pesade." By "loin"
here he means the hollow on each side below the
ribs, — the flanks.

57. (PAGE 63.) Xenophon refers to the phylarch
and hipparch, respectively. See p. 75.

58. (PAGE 64.) See cut on p. 61.

59. (PAGE 65.) The cuirass ordinarily consisted
of two metal plates made to fit the body, one protecting the breast and abdomen, and the other
the back. They were hinged on one side, and
buckled on the other. They were further kept in
place by leathern straps or bands of metal, passing
over the shoulders from behind and fastened in

front and by the belt. About the lower part of
the cuirass was a series of flaps of leather or felt,
covered with metal, but flexible, protecting the
hips and groin without interfering with freedom of
movement (see cuts on pp. 19 and 69). There
were also similar flaps at the right shoulder to
protect the part of the body which was left
exposed when the arm was raised to hurl the
javelin or to strike with the sword. But even
in the time of Xenophon, a sort of scale armour
was not unknown, the metallic scales being fastened to a cuirass of felt. On the frieze of the
Parthenon one of the riders wears a combination of plate and scale armour, the breast and
back being covered by plates which are joined
at the sides by scale armour. Of course all parts
of the cuirass were often elaborately ornamented.
Xenophon's insistence on the point that the
cuirass should be made to fit the individual
reminds one of the conversation reported by him
in the "Memorabilia" (3, 10, 9 ff.) between
Socrates and a cuirass-maker.

60. (PAGE 65.) The neck-piece is rarely seen
in art, but is found on certain reliefs from Pergamon (Altertümer von Pergamon, ii, 43, 44, 2, and
47, 2). It comes up between the shoulder-straps,
and is at the back of the neck, not at the front.
So in the statuette of the Etruscan warrior, called
the Mars of Todi; see Baumeister, taf. lxxxix.

But a cuirass with the neck-piece extending all the way round has been found at Grenoble (Baumeister, p. 2044), and is represented on the coin which serves as the tail-piece to Chapter I (p. 19). It is probable that this piece was an Eastern device, suggested to Xenophon during his campaign in Persia, and not generally adopted in Greece.

61. (PAGE 66.) It is impossible to say what Xenophon meant by a Boeotian helmet. There were two principal types of Greek helmets, — the Corinthian and the Attic, to be seen on the head of Athene on the coins of Corinth and Athens respectively. The Corinthian, having a nose-piece and immovable cheek-pieces, was the more complete protection. The Athenian generally had cheek-pieces, always movable, however, so that they could be turned up, leaving the face free. These do not always appear on the coins. Both helmets protected the nape of the neck. But as Xenophon has provided for the protection of the throat by a special piece rising from the cuirass, he can scarcely mean the Corinthian helmet which covers this part pretty effectually; and his description would conform even less closely to the Attic type.

62. (PAGE 66.) Examples (but not of Greek origin) of this flexible piece of armour have been found at Olympia and at Pergamon (Curtius and Adler, Olympia, tafelband iv; Altertümer von Pergamon, ii, taf. 43). It was made of strips of metal, lapping over each other like the fingers of a mediaeval gauntlet. See also Baumeister, Denkmäler, p. 2028.

63. (PAGE 66.) Greaves were made of elastic metal, lined with felt or leather, and were snapped about the leg below the knee and then fastened behind with straps or buckles. Such a piece is here recommended to fit the right arm; and on the analogy of the leg-greave I suppose that it was intended for the part of the arm below the elbow.

64. (PAGE 67.) That is, the part near the shoulder and the armpit; this is left unprotected by the unfolding of the flaps mentioned above.

65. (PAGE 67.) The armour here prescribed for the horse is not Greek, but Oriental. We find no evidence of its use in Greece in the art or litera-ture of the fifth century. Xenophon, doubtless, became acquainted with it during the Expedition of the Ten Thousand, approved it and desired its introduction into Greece. It was introduced to a limited extent in the fourth century. But there is nothing in art to explain how the thigh-armour of the horse protected the rider's legs.

66. (PAGE 67.) Here the Greek word is ἔποχον; but just before and in chapter seven (see note 42)

the usual word for the cloth, ἐφίππιον, is used. It
is not certain what the difference was between the
two ; but probably, as Schlieben thinks, the ἔποχον
was more extensive ; and was padded or quilted
(see the great Pompeian mosaic of the battle of
Issus) ; perhaps it was continued under the belly.

67. (PAGE 67.) Such boots may be seen on the
frieze of the Parthenon and on the Orvieto vase
(cut facing p. 76).

68. (PAGE 67.) The words "sword," "sabre," and
" scimitar " are used only as approximations here.
The Greek swords of all sorts were much shorter
than ours; and the two latter forms resembled
curved butcher's-knives rather than swords, in our
sense of the word.

69. (PAGE 68.) See the Orvieto vase (cut facing
p. 76).

70. (PAGE 68.) The " Hipparchicus," or " Cavalry General ; " see p. 71.

71. (PAGE 74.) There are only three passages,
and two of them (Iliad, 15, 679; Odyssey, 5,
371) are in similes ; hence they may and doubtless do refer, not to the heroic period in which
the scene of the poem was laid, but to the later
time when the verses were written.   The third is

the only passage in which heroes are actually described as riding on horseback (Iliad, 10, 513) ; but this is in the Dolopeia, universally admitted to be the latest part of the Iliad in order of composition. It cannot, therefore, be accepted as evidence in the face of the general practice of driving, found everywhere else in heroic scenes.

As my book is concerned only with the later practice of riding, there is no need to discuss the very obscure question of the introduction of the horse into Greece, shadowed forth as it may or may not have been by the myths of Pegasus, the Centaurs, Erechtheus, and Poseidon. According to Pietrément (whom I quote at second-hand, having never seen his book, as I remarked in my preface), no fossil remains of horses have been found in Greece ; and the animal was certainly introduced thither, though the route is unknown.

72. (PAGE 76.) The price of the horse branded with the letter Koppa, in Aristophanes' "Clouds," 20. The exact significance of this and other brands is unknown, save that horses thus branded were of more than ordinary value. See cut on p. 184, and its description.

73. (PAGE 84.) See Pliny, N. H. 35, 95 ; Aelian, V. H. 2, 3.

74. (PAGE 85.) Pseudo-Lucian, Dem. Encom., 24 ; Aelian, V. H. 14, 15.

75. (PAGE 85.) Aelian, H. A. 4, 50; Pollux, 2, 69.

76. (PAGE 87.) The description by Vegetius (fifth century) in the "Mulomedicina," 4, 6 (6, 6) is of a particular breed, and that not a Greek one. Isidorus, Origines, 12, 1, 45 (seventh century), and Pollux, 1, 188 ff. (second century) are mere compilers, adding nothing in this matter to the knowledge which we have from other sources.

77. (PAGE 93.) Light may come from another direction. We find now and then that the manes of horses were shorn as a sign of mourning. This was done by Persians on the death of Mardonius (Hdt. 9, 24), and by Greeks on the deaths of Pelopidas and Hephaestion (Plutarch, Pelopidas, 33; Alexander, 72). In the Alcestis of Euripides, 428 ff., the bereaved husband orders all his subjects to shear the manes of their horses.

78. (PAGE 94.) Not a Homeric fashion, however, (see *e.g.* Iliad, 17, 439). It was intermediate between the Heroic and the Classical Age.

79. (PAGE 98.) See Pliny, N. H. 8, 156 f.

80. (PAGE 99.) The horse Xanthus and his mate wept for the death of Patroclus; but their grief was not appreciated by the charioteer Automedon (Iliad, 17, 426 ff.).

81. (PAGE 101.) Our information comes from Plutarch, Life of Alexander, 6; 32; 61; Morals, p. 970 D; Arrian, Anabasis, 5, 14, 4; 19, 4 ff.; Strabo, p. 698; Gellius, 5, 2; Geoponics, 16, 2; Curtius, 6, 5, 18; 9, 3, 23; Pliny, N. H. 8, 154; Aelian, V. H. 2, 3.

82. (PAGE 101.) See Aristophanes, frag. 41, Kock.

ON THE ILLUSTRATIONS.

IN making selections from the antique for the pictures in this book, I have been guided, not so much by the interest or beauty of the originals, considered as works of art, as by their usefulness in explaining or illustrating the various subjects which have been treated in the foregoing pages. So, too, the following brief notes are not written from the point of view of the art-critic, an office to which I do not pretend; but in them I have given the immediate source from which each illustration is taken, the museum or collection in which the object itself is to be seen to-day, and, wherever possible, the time of its production, and the place where it was found. I have mentioned, also, the points in each work which led me to choose it for the purposes of this book. Without too great presumption I may venture to remark that but few, if any, of the Classics, except Homer, have been thus closely and fully illustrated from ancient art. The present attempt may serve to show what an opportunity there is in this direction.

FULL–PAGE ILLUSTRATIONS.

FRONTISPIECE.   Bronze head in the Uffizi, Florence, No. 426 of the bronzes in the collection in that gallery. From a photograph. The work was found near Città Vecchia, and was sent from Rome to Florence in 1585, according to the catalogue of the Uffizi gallery. The time of its production is unknown. Originally there was a bridle on the head ; the mouthpiece of the bit still remains. This head has the ears wide apart, leaving the poll large (see p. 17) ; and it therefore illustrates the type of beauty which gave rise to the term βουκέφαλος (see note 12, p. 125).

PAGE 17.   From the frieze of the Parthenon, a work completed about 440 B. C. under the direction of Phidias (see pp. 84 and 97).   From a photograph in "Masterpieces of Antique Art," by S. Thompson. Although this slab is not in as perfect a state of preservation as are some of the others, yet it has always been among the most admired for the grace, action, and truth to nature of its figures. The horses seem to illustrate exactly the type preferred by Xenophon in his first chapter (see also p. 89). For the costume of the riders see the remarks on p. 163.

PAGE 41. Fragment of a sixth-century monument in honour of an Athenian warrior of a time much earlier than the Persian wars. From "Die Attischen Grabreliefs," Conze, i, taf. 9. The original is in the Barracco collection in Rome; Conze took his engraving from a cast in Strasburg. The complete work was a tall, narrow stele, like the well-known stele of Aristion. On the upper part was represented the dead man, armed probably as a hoplite; only his feet and the butt of his spear remain. Below, in what is called the κρηπίς of the monument, is a young horseman, holding the reins in his left hand and in his right two javelins; he is armed also with a short, straight sword. It should be remembered that the two reins are often represented on the same side in early art, so that this relief does not prove the existence of two sets of reins (see note 53, p. 144). The reins must be supposed to be attached directly to the bit; there is here no representation of branches, but such details are often neglected in art. This rider, however, carries two javelins; and yet Xenophon in his twelfth chapter (p. 68) speaks as if he were

recommending something entirely new in suggest-
ing the use of two javelins instead of one spear.
But the technique of this work shows that the
rider is of a time long before Xenophon; further,
on a number of early vase-paintings (see for
instance pp. 30 and 65), two javelins are carried
by cavaliers.   I am not aware that any explanation has been offered of this apparent contradic-
tion.   When it is remembered, however, that the
Athenians had no regularly organized body of
cavalry before the Persian wars (see p. 75), it
may be thought that after the organization of the
force it was armed merely with one spear; and
that in the transition state before this organization,
hoplites, when mounted for some special purpose,
carried two.   Thus, the present monument may
have represented the dead warrior serving in two
capacities, — on foot and as a mounted hoplite.
It is true that the rider in the Lamptrae relief
(facing p. 68)* carries but one spear; and so the
custom probably varied before the knights were
organized.

PAGE 68.* Part of a fragment of a monument
found in the Attic deme of Lamptrae, and now in
Athens.   From the "Mittheilungen des deutschen
arch. Instituts in Athen," xii, taf. 2.   A work of
perhaps a little after the middle of the sixth
century.   See the remarks just above, and note
that the regular Athenian cavalry did not carry

* Page 98

shields. The rider wears the usual short mantle. The horse is a much better animal than the one represented in the plate just treated; on his gait see p. 141. Another horse is led at the left as the outlines show. This is not uncommon in art.

PAGE 76. From an Attic cylix, or cup, found at Orvieto, in Central Italy, described and illustrated by G. Körte in the "Archäologische Zeitung," 1880, taf. 15. It is now in the Berlin Museum. The picture represents the examination for admission to the Athenian cavalry, the δοκιμασία (see p. 76). At the left, just below the handle of the cup, is a bearded man seated under a tree, with a stylus and a writing-tablet in his hands. In front of him stands a man with a long staff (the cup is here broken). Towards them are approaching three young men, dressed alike, not in armour, but in the usual gala or parade costume of the cavalry, — a chlamys, or short cloak, buckled at the shoulder; a petasus, or broad-brimmed hat; and κόθορνοι, or high riding-boots (actually, the artist has represented these boots only in the case of the second rider). Each brings up his horse by a leading-rein (see note 38, p. 138), not by the bridle (see note 34, p. 136); the bridles in fact are here left to the imagination, and the leading-rein is supposed to be attached to the chin-strap or nose-band. In the cut on p. 39 the bridle-rein

and the leading-rein are distinguished, the thick
dark streak representing the latter.   The horses,
Körte thinks, are not represented in a natural
gait (see p. 141) ; yet perhaps not much evidence
on this point can be got from a representation
of horses moving at a walk (see p. 163).   Each
man carries two javelins (see p. 162).   The horses
have long tails, long forelocks (see p. 32), and
hogged manes (see p. 93).   Behind the first
horse stands a young man (also under a tree),
with a peculiar staff having a crook at the upper
end.   This man may be the hipparch or the
phylarch (see p. 75) of the troop undergoing
examination, for we know that young men were
chosen to these offices.   Finally, behind the
third horse stands a bearded man with a staff of
office.   The two upright bearded men are doubtless the examining committee of the Senate ; the
seated man is their secretary.   The first knight is
actually in course of examination, as his upright
and attentive position shows ; the second is on his
way, the third just starting.   The newly discovered
treatise of Aristotle on the Athenian Constitution
gives us some interesting and in part new information about this examination (chap. 49).   In the
centre of the bottom of the cup is one of the two
hundred mounted bowmen, called the Scythians,
employed by the Athenians as a sort of police
force.

PAGE 83. Head of one of the horses of Selene, the moon goddess, from the eastern pediment of the Parthenon, now in the British Museum. From a photograph in Brunn's "Denkmäler Griechischer und Römischer Skulptur," lief. 38. On the eyes, see p. 83; on the mane, p. 95; and on the Bucephalus type of the head, p. 125.

PAGE 89. From the frieze of the Parthenon, as engraved in "Ancient Marbles in the British Museum," viii, pl. 18, and edited by Hawkins. This group affords a most perfect idea of the type of horse approved by Xenophon (see p. 89). I have remarked, at the end of note 46 (p. 143), upon the soothing gesture of the second rider; every foot of his horse is raised from the ground. The third rider is one of the few on the frieze that wear the cuirass (note 59, p. 150); he has also a helmet of the Attic type with folding cheek-pieces (note 61, p. 152), and wears boots (p. 67). But the fifth rider and horse are the best of all; I quote Hawkins here: "Nothing can exceed the vigour, the life, the animation which pervades the whole horse, bounding from the earth with the very exuberance of animal spirits; the muscular power and elasticity with which he springs from the ground is admirably expressed, as are also the playful pawings of the forelegs and the animated expression of lively impatience in the muscles and positions of the head and neck. Nor

less to be admired are the form and character of
the rider, the easy firmness of his seat, the
perfect confidence in his own powers of command, his entire composure and tranquillity con-
trasted with the sudden and vehement action of
the animal beneath him; and the grace and
precision with which the whole framework of
his body is indicated, and the muscular action
developed."

PAGE 109. The monument of Dexileus, an
Athenian knight, who was born, as the inscription
shows, in 414 B. C., and who fell in battle near
Corinth in 394. His youth may show that this
was his first and last campaign. This monument
is still *in situ* in the Street of Tombs, outside the
Dipylon gate of Athens; near it are the stelae of
others of the family of Dexileus. He is in the act
of slaying a foeman. For the purposes of artistic
effect he is not in armour. His weapon, whether
sword or spear, and the bridle of his horse were
doubtless added in bronze. From a photograph
in my possession; the shadow at the left is caused
by a wooden casing, set about the monument to
preserve it. In the reproduction this casing is
happily omitted.

PAGE 145. Assurbanipal (Sardanapalus), King
of Assyria from 668 to 626 B. C., hunting wild
asses. From a photograph of the alabaster relief
found at Kouyunjik, Nineveh, now in the British

Museum. I have chosen this picture merely to illustrate the way in which the rein was attached to the bit, and the bridle to the branches (see p. 146). In the relief itself (though not in this reproduction) it is perfectly clear that the rein was fastened to the little ring.

ILLUSTRATIONS IN THE TEXT.

PAGE 13. From Panofka's " Bilder Antiker Lebens," iii, 1 ; he took it from Tischbein, " Vas d'Hamilton," i, 47. The painting represents the end of a race ; the pillar indicating the goal. On the attachment of the bits, see p. 146. I have grave doubts about the trustworthiness of this picture, but insert it for its life and action. It must, if a correct reproduction, be a late work.

PAGE 19. Coin of King Patraos of Paeonia, 340–315 B. C. From a cut in " An Illustrated Dictionary to the Anabasis " by Professor J. W. White and the present writer, who took it from Baumeister, p. 2030. It is also illustrated and described by Imhoof-Blumer, " Monnaies Grecs," taf. C. The horseman, who is a Paeonian, wears trousers, and has an extremely large crest to his helmet. From his cuirass seems to rise the neck-piece (note 60, p. 151) ; note also the flaps about his loins (p. 66). The inscription above gives the king's name.

PAGE 20. Painting on an Attic vase now in
Munich, found in the ancient Etruscan city of
Vulci.   From   the   " Archäologische Zeitung,"
xliii, taf. 11.   The scene represents a riding-
lesson, the old man at the right being the master.
A young man rides along leading a second horse
upon which his comrade is about to leap by the
use of a vaulting-pole.   For the sake of symmetry
in the picture the artist may have placed this
person in front of the horse instead of at the side,
where he would naturally stand in taking such a
leap; or it may be thought that he is merely
balancing himself, ready to spring on as soon as
the horse reaches him.   When a cavalryman
mounted by means of his spear, he used only one
hand for the spear (see note 41, p. 139).   Livy
speaks of the use of the spear in leaping suddenly
from a horse (iv, 19, 4).   On the other half of this
vase, not shown in my reproduction, a boy is leading a horse, while the teacher looks on under a
tree, showing that this lesson was given in the
open air.   The riding-master Pheidon, mentioned
in Mnesimachus's comedy of the " Horse-breeder,"
a work of the first half of the fourth century, gave
his lessons in the agora, near the Hermae (see
Athenaeus, 402 F.).   But in another vase-painting
(Daremberg et Saglio, ii, fig. 2717), young riders
are exercising under cover.   It is, therefore,
impossible to say whether the ἱππασία mentioned

by Xenophon at the end of his seventh chapter was in or out of doors. I have translated it riding-ground. In a different work (Memorabilia, iii, 3, 6), Xenophon calls the place ἄμμος (the Latin *harena*), showing that horses were exercised upon sand, not hard ground. The object hanging at the left of our picture is an oil-flask, perhaps the *aryballos* (see below), used in the baths and wrestling-schools. The inscription has nothing to do with the actual scene, but is an example of the custom whereby the ancient vase-painter dedicated, as it were, his work to some friend ; to the name was generally attached the adjective καλός (handsome), as here. On the attachment of the horse's bit, see p. 146.

PAGE 22. A proto-Corinthian lecythos, of the shape sometimes called the *aryballos*, perhaps of the early sixth century. Athletes used such vases to hold their oil (see above). From " Die Griechischen Vasen," Lau, taf. iv, 2. The small size of the rider, compared to his horse, is noteworthy (see p. 95) ; observe also the thick, long mane (p. 94).

PAGE 23. From a vase found at Nola, in Campania; reproduced from Panofka's " Bilder Antiker Lebens," i, 5. A riding-master (see p. 168) is helping a boy to mount. In Plato, Laches, 182 A., riding is mentioned along with gymnastics as proper parts of the education of the

Athenian gentleman. In another place he says:
"We must mount our children on horses in their
earliest youth and take them on horseback to see
war, in order that they may learn to ride; the
horses must not be spirited and warlike, but the
most tractable and yet the swiftest that can be
had.   In this way they will get an excellent view
of what is hereafter to be their business; and if
there is danger they have only to follow their elder
leaders and escape" (Republic, 467 E, Jowett's
translation).   This heroic treatment, it must be
remembered, is Plato's proposal for the ideal state,
and it does not prove that boys were ever actually
taken to see battles by the Athenians.   The great
physician Galen, of the second century A. D.,
advised that boys should begin to learn to ride at
the age of seven (De val. tuend. i, 8; ii, 9).
Such a boy seems to be represented in our picture.
But probably in ancient Athens boys began to ride
between the ages of fourteen and eighteen, which
were the years especially devoted to training in
gymnastics.   At eighteen they were eligible for
the cavalry, and began to learn to use weapons
on horseback.   This picture well illustrates the
method of attaching the bit to the bridle (see
p. 146).

PAGE 26. A coin of King Alexander of Macedon, 498–454 B. C., now in Berlin.   From
Baumeister, p. 950.   Note the large size of the

horse compared to the man (p. 98), his forelock (p. 32), and hogged mane (p. 91 ff.). I have already remarked on the extremely large branches of the bit (p. 148). The rider (a Macedonian of course) wears the short cloak adopted by the Athenian cavalry (p. 163), and the hat called *causia*, differing somewhat from the Athenian petasus (see p. 163). He carries two spears (p. 162).

PAGE 27. Painting on a black-figured vase in the British Museum, from Gerhard's "Auserlesene Vasenbilder," iv, 247. This is a Panathenaic vase, intended as a prize for the winner at the Panathenaic festival, probably at some time in the fourth century. This side of the vase shows the kind of contest for which the prize was given; on the other is the conventional figure of Athene. The rider in this case is not the owner, but a jockey. The owner's name is proclaimed by the man walking ahead, in the words ΔΥΝΕΙΚΕΤΥ: ΗΙΠΟΣ: ΝΙΚΑΙ, that is, "the horse of Dysnicetus is the winner." Behind walks a man carrying the prize, a tripod, on his head. In his left hand he holds a chaplet of victory; this, to my regret, is not shown in the present reproduction.

PAGE 29. A silver coin of Maronea in Thrace, 400–350 B. C. From Head's "Catalogue of the Greek Coins in the British Museum," Thrace, p. 126. This coin shows the leading-rein (note

38, p. 138). The inscription indicates the name of the town.

PAGE 30. From a black-figured amphora in the Hermitage collection, St. Petersburg, illustrated (in outline merely) in the "Comte Rendu de la Commission Impériale Archéologique," 1864, p. 5, from which I take it. The horse is bending his knees to allow the Amazon to mount (see p. 138). The inscription above has not been deciphered.

PAGE 33. From Koepp's "Ueber das Bildnis Alexanders des Grossen," p. 3. A gold medallion from Tarsus, of the time of the Emperor Commodus, in the "Cabinet des médailles," the obverse of which bears a fine head of Alexander the Great. The reverse, in our picture, shows the king hunting a lion. Professor Emerson has suggested (in the "American Journal of Archaeology," 1887, p. 253) that for this medallion was selected the central figures in a bronze group, called the Lion Hunt, by Lysippus, dedicated at Delphi by Craterus (Plutarch, Alexander, 40). In this group were included hunting-dogs and Craterus himself coming up to help. The picture shows the flaps at the shoulders and about the loins, mentioned by Xenophon in his description of the cuirass (p. 66). A leopard's skin serves instead of a cloth (notes 42, p. 140, and 66, p. 153). The inscription means "King Alexander."

PAGE 34. From Panofka's "Bilder Antiker

Lebens," iii, 7 (also in colours, a red-figured vase, in Gerhard's " Auserlesene Vasenbilder," iv, 272). The original, found at Vulci, Italy, is in the Royal Museum of Berlin. The picture shows the muzzle, the use of which is recommended by Xenophon whenever a horse is to be led (p. 31). The young man seems to be trying to avoid the difficulties in leading horses which Xenophon mentions (p. 35). He wears the regular cavalry boots (pp. 67 and 163). To the word ΕΓΡΑΦΣΕΝ, painted in the inscription, is prefixed (on the other side of the vase) the painter's name, Epictetus. On the word ΚΑΛΟΣ, see p. 169. Another picture, showing the muzzle in more detail, will be found in the " Jahrbuch des deutschen Arch. Instituts," 1889, taf. 10.

PAGE 38. A painting on a red-figured vase, somewhat broken, found at Orvieto, now in the Museo Egizio ed Etrusco, Florence; from the " Drittes Hallisches Winckelmannsprogramm," 1879, taf. iii, 2. The moon goddess, Selene, seated on a bridleless horse which is grazing or drinking. This goddess was first represented on horseback, so far as we know, by Phidias on the pedestal of the statue of Olympian Zeus (Pausanias, v, 11, 8). Other female divinities thus appearing in ancient art are Artemis, Aurora, and the Roman goddess of horses, Epona. But examples of mortal women on horseback are per-

haps wanting in the art of Greece proper; not so
in that of Asia (see for example the Heroon of
Gjölbaschi, a work of the fifth century B. C., and
Daremberg et Saglio, ii, p. 751). The Amazons,
to be sure, are frequently found on horseback,
riding like men; other females, whether goddesses
or women, are represented as women ride to-day,
except that, so far as I know, they are seated, not
to the left, but to the right of the horse, as in our
picture.

PAGE 39. Painting on a vase in the Berlin
Museum, found probably at Nola; from the illustration in the "Archäologische Zeitung," 1878, taf.
22, where it is described by C. Robert. In this
picture a young horseman (on his costume see
p. 163) is making his horse throw forward the off
forefoot so as to assume the position described by
the verb ὑποβιβάζεσθαι (see p. 38 and note 37,
p. 137). The motive of this picture and all the
attitudes so closely resemble a group on the west
side of the Parthenon frieze that Robert does not
hesitate to say that the vase must have been
painted in Athens, and that it is one of the rare
instances of a vase-painting copied from work in
stone.   But Brunn, in an article in the same periodical (1880, p. 18) finds a similar motive in
other works; for instance, in the coin of Larissa
(see p. 54 of this book) and in a Roman relief
(mentioned on p. 138).   He concludes that this

was a typical position seen in every riding-school, and hence that there is no proof that our picture was painted in Athens or copied from the Parthenon. Note the method of attachment of the bit (p. 146), and the leading-rein, distinguished from the bridle-rein (p. 163). On the fetlocks, see note 6, p. 122.

PAGE 44. A statuette found in the excavations at Dodona, the ancient seat of the worship of Zeus. It is of the most archaic style of work found there, and may belong to the seventh century B. C. I take the picture from "Dodone et ses ruines," Carapanos, pl. 13, 1, described in vol. i, p. 183. The mane of the horse is very thick and long (see p. 91); the forelock is arranged in a sort of tuft, as in Assyrian reliefs (see for example the plate facing p. 145). A similar arrangement, though not found, I believe, in works of the fifth and early fourth century, appears again in later art; see the frontispiece of this book, and the cuts on pp. 13 and 51. On the bridle, see p. 146. The peculiar shape of the rein (I mean the swallow-tailed look at the middle) is found in some Assyrian reliefs; and on the whole this statuette bears many resemblances to those works.

PAGE 45. From "Peintures de Vases Antiques recueilles par Millin et Millingen: publiés et commentées par S. Reinach," pl. i, 45. A vase in the Malmaison collection in the Louvre, found in

Southern Italy.   The scene represents a contest
at the Panathenaic festival.   This contest is referred to in an Attic inscription of the first part
of the fourth century (C. I. A., ii, 965).   A shield
was set up, and at it riders hurled the javelin while
passing at full gallop.   In our picture the first
rider has already thrown his javelin, which has
broken against the shield and lies on the ground;
the rider is soothing his horse by the means
employed also on the Parthenon frieze (see the
end of note 46, p. 143).   The second rider is
about to hurl his javelin, and the winged figures
above with crown and fillets indicate that he is to
be the winner.   This game originated at Argos,
at the festival of Hera; and the shield went to the
winner (Pindar, Ol. 7, 83; Nem. 10, 22; Hyginus,
170, 273).   On the bits, see p. 146.

PAGE 50.   A bit found on the Acropolis of
Athens, fully described in note 53, p. 145.

PAGE 51.   Bronze statuette found at Herculaneum in 1761.   From an engraving in Duruy's
"Histoire des Grecs," iii, p. 233, where it is taken
from a photograph.   It is also given, in outline, in
the Museo Borbonico, iii, tav. 27.   Now in the
Naples Museum.   Save in the mane and tail, this
horse corresponds closely to the description of
Simon (p. 107 ff.).

PAGE 54.   A silver coin of Larissa, in Thessaly;
from the "Monatsberichte der Königlichen Preus-

sischen Akad. der Wiss.," 1878, taf. 2, 30. Of
the motive, as Brunn understands it, I have spoken
already (p. 174). On the costume of the man, see
p. 163. The inscription gives the name of the place.

PAGE 55. From an engraving in "Schliemann's
Excavations," Schuchhardt, translated by Sellers,
p. 132. A fragment of a vase found in the excavations at Tiryns, and perhaps of the ninth or
tenth century B. C. The animals and the men all
have a wooden look ; but in spite of the stiff legs,
flat belly, huge eyes, and flame-like mane of the
horse, yet the shape of the head and neck of
the horse show that even in this, the most archaic
of the pictures in this book, the artist had before
his mind the type of animal which we see in the
best art (see p. 90). The lines above the horse's
back are not intended for reins, but are part of the
geometrical ornamentation. The men carry each
a shield and a spear, and probably wore the skin
of some animal of which the tail appears dangling
down below. The colouring of this vase is a
lustrous brown on a light yellow ground.

PAGE 60. A bit, fully described on p. 147.

PAGE 61. From Schoene's "Griechische Reliefs," taf. 17. Part of the fragment of a relief
found in Attica, now in the Pinakothek, Munich.
The lower part, here omitted, contains an olive
crown, showing that the relief was set up by a
victor in a ἱππικὸς ἀγών or πομπή, an equestrian

contest or a parade; perhaps he was a hipparch
or phylarch (see p. 75). I have chosen this relief
because it seems to illustrate Xenophon's words
on the proper way to lead a troop of cavalry, if
you wish to make the whole line "a sight well
worth seeing" (p. 64).

PAGE 64. A silver coin of Ichnae, in Macedonia, 500–480 B.C. From the "Catalogue of the
Greek Coins in the British Museum," Macedonia,
p. 76. Note the hogged mane of the horse
(p. 94) and the rider's greaves (note 63, p. 153).
The inscription gives the name of the town.

PAGE 65. An Attic black-figured vase of the
fifth century; from Gerhard's "Vases Étrusques
et Campaniens du Mus. Roy. de Berlin," pl. xii.
The horsemen wear greaves (note 63, p. 153), and
each carries two spears (p. 162); the helmet may
be the type called Boeotian (note 61, p. 152).
The inscriptions at the left and at the right show
that the two men are the Attic heroes, Acamas
and Demophon, sons of Theseus and Phaedra.
Homer does not mention them; but according to
later stories current among the Athenians, they
went to the Trojan war, and Vergil puts Acamas
among the heroes in the Trojan horse. They
appear several times in vase-paintings; and there
were bronze equestrian statues of them on the
Acropolis, as well as a painting of them by Polygnotus at Delphi. The names of their horses are

given in our picture, — Phalius, of the horse at the left, and Calliphora, of that at the right. The first, which was also the name of the charger of Belisarius (Procopius, B. G. i, 18), means that the animal had a white star on his forehead; the second means "handsome legged." The perpendicular inscription between the two animals is a dedication (see p. 169) of the vase to the handsome Onetorides.

PAGE 69. Bronze statuette of Alexander on Bucephalas in the Naples Museum, found at Herculaneum; from the outline engraving in the "Museo Borbonico," iii, 43. Ever since its discovery in 1761, it has been supposed to be a reduced copy from the bronze group by Lysippus, made at Alexander's own order, to represent an incident at the battle on the Granicus in 334 B. C. In this battle the king's helmet was broken by a blow from a sword (Plutarch, Alex. 17); hence he is here represented bare-headed. The entire group, consisting of many figures, was carried to Rome by Metellus (Vell. Pat. i, 11, 3). This horse closely resembles the other (p. 51) found at the same time and place. On the broad brow, see note 12, p. 125; on the cloth, note 42, p. 140; on the bit, p. 149; on the breastplate, p. 67; on the flaps at Alexander's shoulders and loins, p. 66.

PAGE 106. From an engraving in "Antiquités de Bosphore Cimmérien," Reinach, pl. xx. A

repoussé gold ornament, here represented a little
more than half the size of the original, found in
Koul-Oba in the Crimea, now in St. Petersburg.
The scene represents a Scythian horseman hunting
a hare.   On the bit, see p. 146.

PAGE 107.   From " Monuments Grecs publiés
par l'association pour l'encouragement des études
Grecques en France," Nos. 14–16, pl. 5, with a
long description.   The vase, found at Vulci in
Etruria, is now in the Louvre, and was made in
Athens, probably about 450 B. C.   Our picture,
which is painted on the inside of the cup, represents a young cavalryman with curled hair,
through which is passed a red fillet.   He wears a
long mantle, richly made and of some rather stiff
material, instead of the usual short cloak (pp. 163,
171); his petasus (p. 163) is hanging at his back by
a cord which passes round his neck; another cord
hanging on his shoulder served to keep the hat in
place when it was worn on the head.   His boots
are of the usual cavalry pattern (p. 163), and he
carries two javelins (p. 162).   The horse is decid-
edly ugly; he is too thin and bony, and his head
is too long and narrow at the sides to satisfy a
Greek connoisseur.   Yet the artist has not done
badly with the details of the anatomy, the muscles
of the back and hind quarters, the folds where the
fore legs are set on, and with the tail.   The bridle
is merely indicated, but we can see how the bit

was attached (p. 146). The pose of horse and man being one of complete repose, it may be thought that we have here an outpost, doing guard duty, — perhaps in winter, as this might account for the heavy cloak. A good list of vase-paintings of men on horseback will be found in the article from which I have taken the above description.

PAGE 119. From Engelmann and Anderson's " Pictorial Atlas to Homer," plate xiv, 74. From a Panathenaic vase (see p. 171) of the sixth century B. C., found at Camirus in Rhodes. It is better illustrated in Salzmann's " Nécropole de Camiros," pl. 57, as black-figured on an orange ground. The scene represents acrobats perform-ing, and I take the following description from the first book named above : " Two horses are in full gallop in the ring, guided by a single rider, who looks round at an acrobat, who, with the aid of a spring-board, has leaped on the back of his horse, and, with two shields, is performing a martial dance, jumping from one to the other. He is represented as very small on account of the lack of space. Below, between the horses' legs, is another figure (also made small and placed in this strange position for want of space) who is busily engaged in smoothing the sand of the ring with a pick, just as the grooms do with a rake in the modern circus. Behind the horses is a man play-ing on a double flute in front of the spectators,

who are seated on tiers of benches to the left.
They are applauding loudly, and one of them
shouts, 'Bravo, fine tumbling!' (καλῶς τοι
κυβιστεῖτοι). On the right a youth is seen climbing up a pole (with a slanting support at one
side) ; but whether this is another performance or
part of the jockey's display, it is impossible to
determine."

Although we have no evidence of riding in the
Heroic age, as I have remarked above (p. 74 and
note 71, p. 154), yet at the time when the
Homeric poems were composed, riding had
reached such a stage of progress that even acro-
batic performances on horseback were not unknown. One of the Homeric similes to which I
referred in the note just mentioned runs as follows :
" As when a man that well knows how to ride, har-
nesses up four chosen horses, and, springing from
the ground, dashes to the great city along the
public highway; and crowds of men and women
look on in wonder; while he with all confidence,
as his steeds fly on, keeps leaping from one to
another" (Iliad, xv, 679 ff.). Scenes like the
one portrayed in our picture were probably
familiar to the writer of those verses. This performance seems to be taking place in a regular
circus. What has been called a "spring-board"
in the description above quoted seems to me to be
almost exactly like one of those hollow wooden

pedestals on which the helpers in the modern circus stand when they hold out the paper hoops through which the rider is to jump. Of an event in which highly trained horses bore a part an amusing story is told. The luxurious people of Sybaris in Southern Italy had trained their horses to dance to the music of the flute. Their inveterate enemies, the people of Croton, took advantage of this, and having substituted flutes instead of the usual trumpets in their army, suddenly struck up a dancing tune just as a battle was beginning. Thereupon the horses of the Sybarites instantly threw off their riders, and began to skip and dance, and the men of Croton won the battle (Aelian, N. A., xvi, 23). If there is any truth in this story, it shows either that the Greeks of Magna Graecia used cavalry earlier than the people of Greece proper (for Sybaris was destroyed by Croton in 510 B. C., and we have seen that the Athenians had no cavalry before the Persian wars), or else that the event described took place after the return of the Sybarites to the site of their old city, about 450 B. C.

PAGE 157. A silver coin of Potidaea, of about 500 B. C., from the " Catalogue of Coins in the British Museum," Macedonia, p. 99. The rider is Poseidon Hippios, the sea-god here appearing as patron of horses, which, according to the myth, he created. On the size of the horse see p. 98.

PAGE 159. From an amphora illustrated and described in the "Achtes Hallisches Winckelmannsprogramm," 1883. The vase is of the middle of the third century B. C., was found at Ruvi in Apulia, and is now in the Naples Museum. I have taken from it only the figure of a Greek warrior; in the rest of the picture an Eastern king is escaping from him at full speed in a chariot. It is thought that the painting, without referring to any actual historical scene, symbolizes the triumph of Alexander, as representing Greek civilization, over Darius, as the representative of the East.

TAILPIECE. A silver coin of King Pausanias of Macedon, 390–389 B. C., from the "Catalogue of Greek Coins in the British Museum," Macedonia, p. 169. I have spoken above (note 72, p. 155) of the letter Koppa branded upon horses of extraordinary value. On the hindquarter of this horse is branded a caduceus, or staff of Hermes. Other brands are mentioned in Daremberg et Saglio, ii, p. 800. The inscription on this coin gives the king's name.

INDEX.

A CATALOG OF SELECTED DOVER
BOOKS IN ALL FIELDS OF INTEREST

CONCERNING THE SPIRITUAL IN ART, Wassily Kandinsky. Pioneering work by father of abstract art. Thoughts on color theory, nature of art. Analysis of earlier masters. 12 illustrations. 80pp. of text. 5⅜ x 8½.   0-486-23411-8

CELTIC ART: The Methods of Construction, George Bain. Simple geometric techniques for making Celtic interlacements, spirals, Kells-type initials, animals, humans, etc. Over 500 illustrations. 160pp. 9 x 12. (Available in U.S. only.)   0-486-22923-8

AN ATLAS OF ANATOMY FOR ARTISTS, Fritz Schider. Most thorough reference work on art anatomy in the world. Hundreds of illustrations, including selections from works by Vesalius, Leonardo, Goya, Ingres, Michelangelo, others. 593 illustrations. 192pp. 7⅛ x 10¼.   0-486-20241-0

CELTIC HAND STROKE-BY-STROKE (Irish Half-Uncial from "The Book of Kells"): An Arthur Baker Calligraphy Manual, Arthur Baker. Complete guide to creating each letter of the alphabet in distinctive Celtic manner. Covers hand position, strokes, pens, inks, paper, more. Illustrated. 48pp. 8¼ x 11.   0-486-24336-2

EASY ORIGAMI, John Montroll. Charming collection of 32 projects (hat, cup, pelican, piano, swan, many more) specially designed for the novice origami hobbyist. Clearly illustrated easy-to-follow instructions insure that even beginning papercrafters will achieve successful results. 48pp. 8¼ x 11.   0-486-27298-2

BLOOMINGDALE'S ILLUSTRATED 1886 CATALOG: Fashions, Dry Goods and Housewares, Bloomingdale Brothers. Famed merchants' extremely rare catalog depicting about 1,700 products: clothing, housewares, firearms, dry goods, jewelry, more. Invaluable for dating, identifying vintage items. Also, copyright-free graphics for artists, designers. Co-published with Henry Ford Museum & Greenfield Village. 160pp. 8¼ x 11.   0-486-25780-0

THE ART OF WORLDLY WISDOM, Baltasar Gracian. "Think with the few and speak with the many," "Friends are a second existence," and "Be able to forget" are among this 1637 volume's 300 pithy maxims. A perfect source of mental and spiritual refreshment, it can be opened at random and appreciated either in brief or at length. 128pp. 5⅜ x 8½.   0-486-44034-6

JOHNSON'S DICTIONARY: A Modern Selection, Samuel Johnson (E. L. McAdam and George Milne, eds.). This modern version reduces the original 1755 edition's 2,300 pages of definitions and literary examples to a more manageable length, retaining the verbal pleasure and historical curiosity of the original. 480pp. 5³⁄₁₆ x 8¼.   0-486-44089-3

ADVENTURES OF HUCKLEBERRY FINN, Mark Twain, Illustrated by E. W. Kemble. A work of eternal richness and complexity, a source of ongoing critical debate, and a literary landmark, Twain's 1885 masterpiece about a barefoot boy's journey of self-discovery has enthralled readers around the world. This handsome clothbound reproduction of the first edition features all 174 of the original black-and-white illustrations. 368pp. 5⅜ x 8½.   0-486-44322-1

STICKLEY CRAFTSMAN FURNITURE CATALOGS, Gustav Stickley and L. & J. G. Stickley. Beautiful, functional furniture in two authentic catalogs from 1910. 594 illustrations, including 277 photos, show settles, rockers, armchairs, reclining chairs, bookcases, desks, tables. 183pp. 6½ x 9¼.   0-486-23838-5

AMERICAN LOCOMOTIVES IN HISTORIC PHOTOGRAPHS: 1858 to 1949, Ron Ziel (ed.). A rare collection of 126 meticulously detailed official photographs, called "builder portraits," of American locomotives that majestically chronicle the rise of steam locomotive power in America. Introduction. Detailed captions. xi+ 129pp. 9 x 12.   0-486-27393-8

AMERICA'S LIGHTHOUSES: An Illustrated History, Francis Ross Holland, Jr. Delightfully written, profusely illustrated fact-filled survey of over 200 American lighthouses since 1716. History, anecdotes, technological advances, more. 240pp. 8 x 10¾.
0-486-25576-X

TOWARDS A NEW ARCHITECTURE, Le Corbusier. Pioneering manifesto by founder of "International School." Technical and aesthetic theories, views of industry, economics, relation of form to function, "mass-production split" and much more. Profusely illustrated. 320pp. 6⅛ x 9¼. (Available in U.S. only.)   0-486-25023-7

HOW THE OTHER HALF LIVES, Jacob Riis. Famous journalistic record, exposing poverty and degradation of New York slums around 1900, by major social reformer. 100 striking and influential photographs. 233pp. 10 x 7⅞.   0-486-22012-5

FRUIT KEY AND TWIG KEY TO TREES AND SHRUBS, William M. Harlow. One of the handiest and most widely used identification aids. Fruit key covers 120 deciduous and evergreen species; twig key 160 deciduous species. Easily used. Over 300 photographs. 126pp. 5⅜ x 8½.   0-486-20511-8

COMMON BIRD SONGS, Dr. Donald J. Borror. Songs of 60 most common U.S. birds: robins, sparrows, cardinals, bluejays, finches, more–arranged in order of increasing complexity. Up to 9 variations of songs of each species.
Cassette and manual 0-486-99911-4

ORCHIDS AS HOUSE PLANTS, Rebecca Tyson Northen. Grow cattleyas and many other kinds of orchids–in a window, in a case, or under artificial light. 63 illustrations. 148pp. 5⅜ x 8½.   0-486-23261-1

MONSTER MAZES, Dave Phillips. Masterful mazes at four levels of difficulty. Avoid deadly perils and evil creatures to find magical treasures. Solutions for all 32 exciting illustrated puzzles. 48pp. 8¼ x 11.   0-486-26005-4

MOZART'S DON GIOVANNI (DOVER OPERA LIBRETTO SERIES), Wolfgang Amadeus Mozart. Introduced and translated by Ellen H. Bleiler. Standard Italian libretto, with complete English translation. Convenient and thoroughly portable–an ideal companion for reading along with a recording or the performance itself. Introduction. List of characters. Plot summary. 121pp. 5¼ x 8½.   0-486-24944-1

FRANK LLOYD WRIGHT'S DANA HOUSE, Donald Hoffmann. Pictorial essay of residential masterpiece with over 160 interior and exterior photos, plans, elevations, sketches and studies. 128pp. 9¼ x 10¾.   0-486-29120-0

THE CLARINET AND CLARINET PLAYING, David Pino. Lively, comprehensive work features suggestions about technique, musicianship, and musical interpretation, as well as guidelines for teaching, making your own reeds, and preparing for public performance. Includes an intriguing look at clarinet history. "A godsend," *The Clarinet,* Journal of the International Clarinet Society. Appendixes. 7 illus. 320pp. 5⅜ x 8½. 0-486-40270-3

HOLLYWOOD GLAMOR PORTRAITS, John Kobal (ed.). 145 photos from 1926-49. Harlow, Gable, Bogart, Bacall; 94 stars in all. Full background on photographers, technical aspects. 160pp. 8⅜ x 11¼. 0-486-23352-9

THE RAVEN AND OTHER FAVORITE POEMS, Edgar Allan Poe. Over 40 of the author's most memorable poems: "The Bells," "Ulalume," "Israfel," "To Helen," "The Conqueror Worm," "Eldorado," "Annabel Lee," many more. Alphabetic lists of titles and first lines. 64pp. 5³/₁₆ x 8¼. 0-486-26685-0

PERSONAL MEMOIRS OF U. S. GRANT, Ulysses Simpson Grant. Intelligent, deeply moving firsthand account of Civil War campaigns, considered by many the finest military memoirs ever written. Includes letters, historic photographs, maps and more. 528pp. 6⅛ x 9¼. 0-486-28587-1

POE ILLUSTRATED: Art by Doré, Dulac, Rackham and Others, selected and edited by Jeff A. Menges. More than 100 compelling illustrations, in brilliant color and crisp black-and-white, include scenes from "The Raven," "The Pit and the Pendulum," "The Gold-Bug," and other stories and poems. 96pp. 8⅜ x 11. 0-486-45746-X

RUSSIAN STORIES/RUSSKIE RASSKAZY: A Dual-Language Book, edited by Gleb Struve. Twelve tales by such masters as Chekhov, Tolstoy, Dostoevsky, Pushkin, others. Excellent word-for-word English translations on facing pages, plus teaching and study aids, Russian/English vocabulary, biographical/critical introductions, more. 416pp. 5⅜ x 8½. 0-486-26244-8

PHILADELPHIA THEN AND NOW: 60 Sites Photographed in the Past and Present, Kenneth Finkel and Susan Oyama. Rare photographs of City Hall, Logan Square, Independence Hall, Betsy Ross House, other landmarks juxtaposed with contemporary views. Captures changing face of historic city. Introduction. Captions. 128pp. 8¼ x 11. 0-486-25790-8

NORTH AMERICAN INDIAN LIFE: Customs and Traditions of 23 Tribes, Elsie Clews Parsons (ed.). 27 fictionalized essays by noted anthropologists examine religion, customs, government, additional facets of life among the Winnebago, Crow, Zuni, Eskimo, other tribes. 480pp. 6⅛ x 9¼. 0-486-27377-6

TECHNICAL MANUAL AND DICTIONARY OF CLASSICAL BALLET, Gail Grant. Defines, explains, comments on steps, movements, poses and concepts. 15-page pictorial section. Basic book for student, viewer. 127pp. 5⅜ x 8½. 0-486-21843-0

THE MALE AND FEMALE FIGURE IN MOTION: 60 Classic Photographic Sequences, Eadweard Muybridge. 60 true-action photographs of men and women walking, running, climbing, bending, turning, etc., reproduced from a rare 19th-century masterpiece. vi + 121pp. 9 x 12. 0-486-24745-7

LIGHT AND SHADE: A Classic Approach to Three-Dimensional Drawing, Mrs. Mary P. Merrifield. Handy reference clearly demonstrates principles of light and shade by revealing effects of common daylight, sunshine, and candle or artificial light on geometrical solids. 13 plates. 64pp. 5³/₈ x 8¹/₂. 0-486-44143-1

ASTROLOGY AND ASTRONOMY: A Pictorial Archive of Signs and Symbols, Ernst and Johanna Lehner. Treasure trove of stories, lore, and myth, accompanied by more than 300 rare illustrations of planets, the Milky Way, signs of the zodiac, comets, meteors, and other astronomical phenomena. 192pp. 8³/₈ x 11. 0-486-43981-X

JEWELRY MAKING: Techniques for Metal, Tim McCreight. Easy-to-follow instructions and carefully executed illustrations describe tools and techniques, use of gems and enamels, wire inlay, casting, and other topics. 72 line illustrations and diagrams. 176pp. 8¹/₄ x 10⁷/₈. 0-486-44043-5

MAKING BIRDHOUSES: Easy and Advanced Projects, Gladstone Califf. Easy-to-follow instructions include diagrams for everything from a one-room house for bluebirds to a forty-two-room structure for purple martins. 56 plates; 4 figures. 80pp. 8³/₄ x 6³/₈. 0-486-44183-0

LITTLE BOOK OF LOG CABINS: How to Build and Furnish Them, William S. Wicks. Handy how-to manual, with instructions and illustrations for building cabins in the Adirondack style, fireplaces, stairways, furniture, beamed ceilings, and more. 102 line drawings. 96pp. 8³/₄ x 6³/₈. 0-486-44259-4

THE SEASONS OF AMERICA PAST, Eric Sloane. From "sugaring time" and strawberry picking to Indian summer and fall harvest, a whole year's activities described in charming prose and enhanced with 79 of the author's own illustrations. 160pp. 8¹/₄ x 11. 0-486-44220-9

THE METROPOLIS OF TOMORROW, Hugh Ferriss. Generous, prophetic vision of the metropolis of the future, as perceived in 1929. Powerful illustrations of towering structures, wide avenues, and rooftop parks–all features in many of today's modern cities. 59 illustrations. 144pp. 8¹/₄ x 11. 0-486-43727-2

THE PATH TO ROME, Hilaire Belloc. This 1902 memoir abounds in lively vignettes from a vanished time, recounting a pilgrimage on foot across the Alps and Apennines in order to "see all Europe which the Christian Faith has saved." 77 of the author's original line drawings complement his sparkling prose. 272pp. 5³/₈ x 8¹/₂. 0-486-44001-X

THE HISTORY OF RASSELAS: Prince of Abissinia, Samuel Johnson. Distinguished English writer attacks eighteenth-century optimism and man's unrealistic estimates of what life has to offer. 112pp. 5³/₈ x 8¹/₂. 0-486-44094-X

A VOYAGE TO ARCTURUS, David Lindsay. A brilliant flight of pure fancy, where wild creatures crowd the fantastic landscape and demented torturers dominate victims with their bizarre mental powers. 272pp. 5³/₈ x 8¹/₂. 0-486-44198-9

Paperbound unless otherwise indicated. Available at your book dealer, online at **www.doverpublications.com**, or by writing to Dept. GI, Dover Publications, Inc., 31 East 2nd Street, Mineola, NY 11501. For current price information or for free catalogs (please indicate field of interest), write to Dover Publications or log on to **www.doverpublications.com** and see every Dover book in print. Dover publishes more than 400 books each year on science, elementary and advanced mathematics, biology, music, art, literary history, social sciences, and other areas.